Saffron Fascists

India's Hindu Nationalist Rulers

Pieter Friedrich

Published 2020 by Pieter Friedrich.

Saffron Fascists: India's Hindu Nationalist Rulers.

Copyright © 2020 by Pieter Friedrich. All rights reserved. No part of this publication may be reproduced, stored in a retrieval system, or transmitted in any form or by any means (digital, electronic, mechanical, photocopied, recorded, or otherwise) or conveyed via the internet or a website without prior written permission of the publisher, except in the case of brief quotations embodied in critical books, articles, or reviews.

Cover photos taken by Pieter Friedrich.

Front cover: Saffronites march in Rishikesh, Uttarakhand.

Back cover: BJP flag flies in Goa.

Inquiries should be addressed to:
pieterfriedrich.com

ISBN: 9798675702435

— TABLE OF CONTENTS —

1. World Hindu Congress: Why Were Some Indian-Americans Protesting Against RSS?
2. Disaster for Democracy: How The Modi Wave Flooded India With Fascism
3. How India's Ruling Party Mobilizes Indian-Americans to Win Elections
4. BJP May Have Expelled Sunita Gaur, But It Has Always Rewarded Communal Violence
5. Cultural Malware: The Rise of India's RSS
6. Pulwama: A Present Moment In The Longer Kashmir Story
7. Jammu and Kashmir Loses "Special Status": The Hindu Nationalist Agenda
8. Socializing With The RSS: German Diplomat's "Direct Contact" Approach?
9. Ayodhya: A Symbol of The Rule of Lawlessness
10. US Election: Why Tulsi Gabbard's "Hindutva" Link Deserves Scrutiny
11. The Princess of the RSS and Me
12. Looming Threat of Genocide In India

Acknowledgements

About the Author

— 1 —
World Hindu Congress: Why Were Some Indian-Americans Protesting Against RSS?

15 September 2018

As nine-year-old Hardit Singh joined a march to protest the Second World Hindu Congress held from 7-9 September at the Westin Hotel in suburban Chicago, he searched for words to articulate the caste system.

"They have like four different — you know how they have like temples, and kings, and leaders, and then they have this tower," said Hardit. "It's like Egyptians. Like in a pyramid." As he gesticulated, trying to wrap his mind around the system by speaking with his hands, he grasped that caste is connected to inequalities in power and wealth distribution. "Who gets the less money and who gets the most money. Like the kings, they're at the top. And the poor, they're at the bottom or not even in the thing. There's like four stages. I don't remember all of them, but the last one is separated into a Touchable and an Untouchable."

"Sikhs do not support that," concluded the turbaned young Sikh. "We think everyone is equal. The kings and the poor are all together. They're one thing on this earth."

Marching near Hardit was 26-year-old Gohar from Illinois, who explained that they were protesting the presence of the RSS at the Congress. "They degrade human lives," said Gohar. "There are so many Sikhs and so many Dalits who are living in fear." Gesturing to Hardit, he said, "He's Sikh, and I'm Muslim. We're marching together against brutality. We just don't want killings." Walking alongside was Hardit's grandfather, Gurnam Singh from Virginia, who added, "Christians are also with us."

Controversy began swirling around the Congress shortly after Rashtriya Swayamsevak Sangh (RSS) Sarsanghchalak (Supreme Leader) Mohan Bhagwat was announced as the keynote speaker. Representative Tulsi Gabbard of Hawaii, the first Hindu elected to US Congress, was originally scheduled to chair the event. She resigned, however, after calling the Congress a "platform for partisan politics in India" in a letter to Abhaya Asthana, president of Vishwa Hindu Parishad of America (VHPA), the host organization.

Reports also circulated that Swami Vigyananand, the Vishwa Hindu Parishad of India (VHP) Joint General Secretary who conceived and organized the Congress, once praised his organization's controversial "trishul distribution" program, stating, "You can't kill with the trishul but symbols and ideas are interconnected by the law of association. When the mind gets ready, everything is possible."

More recently, a speaker in the Congress's education channel, Sankrant Sanu, made headlines last month after describing critics of the RSS role in Kerala flood relief as "cockroaches," a term infamously used for the Tutsi victims of the 1994 Rwandan Genocide. On the inaugural day of the Congress, Sanu declared, "India needs to be declared an official Hindu State."

Such demands prompted protestors to turn out en masse on the second and third days of the Congress. "They want to convert everybody," warned Mohammad from Chicago. "They want to make India a Hindu nation. They are saying that what they are doing is for Hindu people, but Hindu religion doesn't in any way promote terrorism, Hindu religion doesn't support killing, Hindu religion doesn't support pushing the minorities. Hindu religion is good, but these people are trying to bring extreme values."

Prominent speakers at the Congress, who knew it would be protested, presented protestors as anti-Hindu. A week before the event, Indian-American author Rajiv Malhotra released a video claiming it was "being attacked." Interpreting the "vicious attacks" as a campaign "started by Indian leftists in the United States," he suggested protests were an assault on the rights of Hindus to practice their religion. "There is absolutely no reason why Hindus should be ashamed," said Malhotra. "There is really no reason why a World Hindu Congress would be a bad idea."

Protestors like Mohammad, however, countered Malhotra's suggestion that they were against a Hindu religious gathering. "We are not protesting against Hindus," he said. "We are protesting against the RSS and the VHP who are the main chief guests for this conference. They are the people behind the whole bloodshed in India." That refrain was echoed again and again by protestors. "They're pretending this is a faith conference, but it's not," said Protiti from Chicago, adding, "They're preaching hatred against minorities." An elderly Sikh man said, "RSS has a convention here. We are not protesting against Hindus. We are protesting against RSS." All three held the same sign: "RSS is a threat to India."

Nearby, Ahmed from Indiana held a sign reading "RSS kills Christians, burns churches." Commenting on the Congress, he said, "They're trying to make it a political philosophy that, in order to be a true Indian, you have to be a Hindu…. Nothing's wrong with being a Hindu. I'm protesting the idea that, in order to be an Indian, which I am, you have to be a Hindu, which I'm not. It's a protest against Hindu nationalism." Adding that "there's a lot of nationalism based on religion throughout the world," he said it should be opposed in all forms and that "even Muslim nationalism is not something that should be encouraged." However, he argued the need of the hour was to stand against the RSS.

The same message galvanized other protestors. Daljit Singh from California, dressed as a Nihang, stood on a grassy slope near the sign to the Westin Hotel. Displaying a sign reading "RSS out of India," he declared, "They're terrorists. They're more dangerous than anybody else. They killed Sikhs in 1984. They killed Muslims in Gujarat. They killed Christians in Odisha." Daljit was confused as to why Bhagwat was allowed into the country. "They killed thousands of people in India. I don't know why they are here. They try to do here the same thing they did in India. We don't want them to kill our people here." Standing on the sidewalk, Davinder Singh of Virginia held a banner reading "end Brahmin theocracy: save India from fascism." He warned, "RSS is a terrorist. Sanatan Sanstha is a terrorist. They attack all the peoples."

Pawan Singh, also from Virginia, carried a sign reading: "Quit killing humans to protect unholy cows."

As the protestors concluded their first day of protests with a march around the hotel property, Pawan stated, "I am here to raise my voice against the terrorist forces of Hindutva who are trying to corrupt the mainstream American institutions." He claimed Hindutva — the political philosophy which unites the RSS and VHP — is being exported to America, warning, "Terroristic forces of Hindutva, including Mohan Bhagwat, have come here to legitimize the genocides of minorities that they have committed." He suggested that atrocities may have occurred in secret, stating, "There are many more that we do not even know of because most of the media is under strict control of the Indian government which is essentially being run by RSS."

While protestors displayed a banner reading "prosecute Mohan Bhagwat for crimes against humanity," the RSS chief took the stage at the Congress to state, "We even allow the pests to live." Claiming that "you have to tackle" the "people who may oppose us," he called for centralization of Hindus under the RSS banner. Although lions and tigers aren't know for moving in packs, he argued, "Even that lion or a royal Bengal tiger, who is the king of the jungle, if he is alone, wild dogs can invade and destroy him."

Bhagwat did not specify if the protestors were one of the intended targets of his "wild dogs" terminology. What was obvious, however, was that "dogs," "cockroaches," and "pests" — that is, terminology typically applied to vermin — was recurrent rhetoric employed to describe those opposed to the RSS both at the Congress and in the weeks leading up to it.

Hundreds of protestors from all walks of life, religions, and nationalities rallied and marched for hours over two days of protest. Dozens of children were present, including one girl of perhaps six-years-old who briefly led chants of "RSS, go away." Both days of protest concluded with distribution of *langar* [free community meals] by the Sikhs. Protestor after protestor reiterated that they were protesting the RSS, not Hinduism.

Nevertheless, Congress speaker Sankrant Sanu, who imitated Malhotra by releasing a video about the "attack" on the event, concluded, "These are very, very radical, extremist hate groups that cannot tolerate the Indian traditions and the Hindu traditions which we talk about in a positive light. So I would ignore the noise."

If we are to go by the words of nine-year-old Hardit Singh, however, these noisemakers were raising their voices for a radical equality. An equality in which rich and poor, high and low, king and peasant are all considered to be on the same level. That might explain why another one of the banners carried by protestors declared, "No human is untouchable: reject caste system."

Originally published by The Citizen [TheCitizen.in].

— 2 —
Disaster for Democracy: How The Modi Wave Flooded India With Fascism

28 May 2019

"In the west, we have labels," commented journalist François Gautier on WION TV, during a panel about the results of India's 2019 general election. "Right, left. Far-right, far-left. We keep applying them to India, where they're not applicable. We cannot apply to India labels we use in the West. To say that the BJP is far-right is completely wrong."

The election was over. The Bharatiya Janata Party (BJP) had won a resounding victory, seizing power once again, with a seat-count in India's *Lok Sabha* that surpassed even its decisive showing in the 2014 elections. Meanwhile, Gautier — described by India's *National Herald* as a French-born "BJP cheerleader" — was speaking truth. The BJP is not *far-right*. But it *is* authoritarian and fascist.

Moments after Gautier spoke, WION's political editor Kartikeya Sharma shed some light on how the BJP may have defeated the opposition: it has infrastructural strength. It is backed by hordes of apparatchiks. "People who are not married, who don't have families, who have dedicated their lives completely to the party," said Sharma. "They land up in a state two years before [the election]. They are living in rented apartments. Along with them, they have an army of youngsters. This is the way. How are you going to compete with that kind of a thing?"

Indeed, fueled by such fanaticism, the organizational power of the *Modi wave* (a term coined to describe the tsunami of support for BJP Prime Minister Narendra Modi) has floated a second BJP victory. India is now on the brink of another five years of subjugation to an authoritarian regime. By 2024, the country will have endured a full decade of BJP rule.

I joined Sharma, Gautier and others on WION to offer my take on the election. "This is a disaster for democracy," I began. "We have to remember that democracy doesn't just mean taking two seconds to push a button once every five years and pick somebody to rule the country. Democracy's actually about the society. It's more than the act of voting. It's about democratic rights, and those democratic rights are in short supply in India today. We can see that India is fast becoming what it has already progressed far along the path towards becoming, which is an organized, centralized, authoritarian democracy — which is fascism."

That's when WION cut my mike and severed the interview. "This is not even acceptable that India is becoming an authoritarian state," responded Sharma. "India is one postcolonial nation which has very successfully demonstrated its ability to transition from one regime to another regime through peaceful elections. I think this comment is unacceptable."

The irony that fascism involves restricting free speech only to "acceptable" answers was lost on him. However, Sharma's choice of the word *regime* — which is generally defined as an authoritarian government — was deeply appropriate.

Last year, an Indian high school teacher was arrested for writing on Facebook, "Voting for Modi is like garlanding a dog." Perhaps such rhetoric is neither the most respectful nor the most constructive way to promote dialogue about the country's political problems. Yet the arrest exemplifies the nature of life under the Modi regime, where expressing discontent, contempt and especially dissent can land an Indian citizen behind bars.

"India's claim to democracy, rather as the world's largest functional democracy, solely rests on its record of regularly held elections," notes jailed Dalit activist Anand Teltumbde. "Although they are more of a ritual observed with massive money and muscle power than the expression of the will of the people, they have sustained the illusion of democracy." Teltumbde argues that "the *de jure* democracy has always been *de facto* plutocracy, the rule of the money bags." He concludes that it was only "a matter of time" before that plutocracy would become exactly what I told WION it was — "an organized, centralized, authoritarian democracy, which is what fascism is."

The emergence of India as a fascist nation ruled by the BJP with Modi as its figurehead is no surprise considering the origins of the BJP. Nor is it a surprise considering the identity of those unmarried, fanatically devoted party workers and their *army of youngsters* who provide the BJP's infrastructural base. Nor is it a surprise considering the history of Modi himself.

Milestones marking the route to the 23 May 2019 results were laid both a century and a half-century ago.

In 1925, the Rashtriya Swayamsevak Sangh (RSS) was formed. A paramilitary force, uniformed and armed, it was dedicated to the idea that all Indians collectively constitute a *Hindu race*; committed to basing the entirety of Indian society, culture and politics on religion; devoted to the notion that only a *race traitor* would vote for anyone but a *Hindu nationalist*; and convinced that it was *treason* against the *mother nation* for an Indian to be anything but a Hindu.

The second milestone happened in 1971, when Narendra Modi joined the RSS as a *pracharak* — a full-time worker sworn to celibacy.

Modi joined in Ahmedabad, the largest city (and then capital) of Gujarat. Modi's home state, Gujarat, lies just north of Maharashtra, the state in which the RSS was founded and in which it maintains its headquarters. At the time, M. S. Golwalkar was nearing the end of his tenure as the RSS's longest-serving and most influential leader. Golwalkar had just excited controversy with a keynote speech at a 1968 RSS rally in Ahmedabad, in which he demanded that India be declared a Hindu *rashtra* (nation). The following year, his petition was sealed in blood when the RSS led riots that left over 400 Muslims dead.

When Golwalkar died in 1973, the RSS was just becoming a political force and Modi was just beginning his public life. In 1980, the RSS founded the BJP as its political wing. Its principal apparatchiks were drawn from the ranks of RSS *pracharaks*. Thus, in 1987 — only two years after another series of riots in Ahmedabad — the RSS assigned Modi to help build the new party.

For months, beginning in February 1985, mobs led by members of the RSS and BJP first attacked lower caste communities and then Muslims. Survivors accuse even the police of joining in the violence, which left hundreds dead. Modi was definitely present in Gujarat during the violence. His role, however, remains unknown. Yet his work within the BJP soon precipitated even deadlier riots.

In the early 1990s, Modi began to validate the party's religious nationalist credentials and emerged as a key organizer of its *Ram janmabhoomi* (Ram's birthplace) campaign.

After Golwalkar founded the Vishwa Hindu Parishad

(VHP) as the RSS's religious wing, the VHP initiated an aggressive movement to reclaim the site where the mythological figure Ram was supposedly born. On that site, they insisted, now stood the sixteenth-century Babri mosque. Claiming that the mosque was built following the demolition of a Ram temple, they demanded the temple be rebuilt.

Recognizing the political potential of this move, the BJP joined the VHP's campaign and adopted the construction of the Ram temple as a plank of the party's agenda. In 1990, BJP President L. K. Advani began a *Ram rath yatra* (Ram chariot procession), criss-crossing India in a minibus decked out as a chariot. He was trailed by thousands of *kar sevaks* (volunteers) from the RSS, VHP and other affiliated groups.

Violence, unsurprisingly, plagued the procession. Riots broke out along the way. Hundreds died in conflicts between Hindus and Muslims. Yet this seemed to prove a successful strategy for the BJP. Despite not actually securing power, they performed exceptionally well in the 1991 general elections. In 1992, however, the movement spun out of control.

In December of that year, Advani headlined a rally outside the Babri mosque. He was joined by Murli Manohar Joshi, who had succeeded him as BJP president. As they spoke, the 150,000 strong crowd moved towards the mosque and began to tear it down. The demolition quickly devolved into a massacre. Nationwide riots, lasting for months, left up to 3,000 Muslims dead.

When India's central government briefly banned both the VHP and the RSS, Modi joined Joshi on a trip to the US. They were greeted on arrival by Suresh Jani of New Jersey, who had in 1991 — on Advani's orders — co-founded the Overseas Friends of the BJP (OFBJP) to counter the negative international press the party was receiving as a result of its *Ram janmabhoomi* campaign. During his US tour, Modi stayed with Jani, as well as with Bharat Barai of Indiana, who was then a governing council member of VHP America.

Back in India, Modi swiftly advanced up the BJP hierarchy. By 1995, he was working out of the national party headquarters in New Delhi. He did not, however, forget his friends in the OFBJP, returning to the US for another tour in 1997. When the BJP emerged victorious in the 1998 general election, he was rewarded with the powerful position of party organizing secretary.

Then he got his hands on real political power.

In October 2001, Gujarat's chief minister Keshubhai Patel was in failing health and had lost his party's political confidence. He resigned. Modi was appointed as his replacement. Thus, the backroom apparatchik — unmarried, with no family, whose life was wholly dedicated to the party — assumed his first ever political office. For four months, he remained an unelected executive. Finally, on 24 February 2002, he won a seat in the Gujarat legislative assembly.

Three days after the election, carnage engulfed Gujarat.

On 27 February, a train was set on fire in the city of Godhra. The passengers were mostly Hindu pilgrims returning to Gujarat from a journey to the *Ram janmabhoomi*. Fifty-nine people (including women and children) died in the blaze.

Modi immediately labelled the conflagration an act of terrorism and blamed it on Pakistan's Inter-Services Intelligence (ISI). That day, his government transported the charred bodies over 100 kilometers from Godhra to

Ahmedabad. Footage of the uncovered corpses was televised before they were handed over to the VHP. With BJP backing, the VHP launched a state-wide shutdown on the 28th. Then the blood began to flow.

For three days, mobs ran rampage throughout the state. Over a dozen cities witnessed major incidents of violence. By the end, up to 2,000 (or more) Muslims lay dead.

Ten years later, a special investigation team (SIT) submitted a report to the Supreme Court. It concluded that there was "not enough evidence" to prosecute Modi for involvement in the pogrom. Indeed, there was little direct evidence proving that he sanctioned the violence — although there was no exculpatory evidence either. There was, however, a mountain of circumstantial evidence.

Eyewitnesses claimed that the attackers were armed with voter lists naming Muslim victims. Witnesses identified BJP state legislator Maya Kodnani as a leader of the assailants and even claimed that she had issued weapons and given orders. Phone records later showed that she was at the scene of the crime and in frequent contact with police and government officials, including Modi's office.

A few months after the pogrom, BJP state minister Haren Pandya told *Outlook* magazine that he — along with other state and police officials — was called to a meeting at Modi's home on the night of the 27th and ordered to stand down so that the mobs could "vent their frustration." Sanjiv Bhatt, a high-ranking police officer, later made the same claim. Survivors say that, when they appealed to police, they were sometimes told by officers, "We have no orders to save you." Witnesses claim police even fired on victims.

Pandya was murdered in 2003. "My husband's assassination was a political murder," asserts his wife. In

2005, his alleged assassin was murdered. BJP state minister Amit Shah — a confidante of Modi's — was accused of orchestrating the assassin's killing after hiring him to murder Pandya.

In 2007, *Tehelka* magazine conducted a sting operation. Speaking with over a dozen perpetrators of the pogrom, they secretly filmed them not only confessing to their involvement but implicating Modi. Interviewees included a BJP state legislator as well as leaders of the RSS and VHP. "He had given us three days to do whatever we could," said legislator Haresh Bhatt, describing Modi. "After three days, he asked us to stop and everything came to a halt … We had three days and did what we had to in those three days."

The evidence was enough to convince the British and American governments to turn their backs on Modi. In 2002, the UK imposed a diplomatic boycott on him, forbidding its officials to deal directly with the Gujarati government. In 2005, the US denied him a visa after he was invited to speak at an Indian diaspora event in Florida.

What most politicians would have interpreted as a nail in the coffin of their political career, Modi and his supporters instead perceived as laying a firm foundation for his future. In the US, Bharat Barai set to work promoting Modi within the Indian-American diaspora. Rather than *the butcher of Gujarat*, he was cast as an economic messiah who introduced the world to the *Gujarat model of development*. Every Gujarat Day, beginning in May 2007, Barai began hosting video conferences in which Modi addressed the diaspora.

Meanwhile, in India, *saffron terror* — a phrase coined to describe terrorism perpetrated by the RSS or its ideological affiliates — was on the rise.

In 2006, a bombing at a Muslim cemetery in Malegaon,

Maharashtra killed forty. In 2007, someone planted a bomb aboard the Samjhauta Express, a train running between Delhi and Lahore. Seventy people, mostly Pakistanis, died. A bombing at the Mecca mosque in Hyderabad killed sixteen. Then a bombing at a Muslim shrine in Ajmer, Rajasthan claimed the lives of two. In 2008, another bombing in Malegaon killed nine. As the investigation into the attacks developed, evidence implicated Swami Aseemanand (an RSS *pracharak*), Sadhvi Pragya Thakur (a leader of RSS-affiliated groups), and a number of other Hindu nationalist activists. In a filmed confession, Aseemanand not only named Thakur, but claimed the violence was directly sanctioned by RSS head Mohan Bhagwat.

Back in the US, as Barai continued to help Modi grow in popularity, Suresh Jani became president of the OFBJP. Fifteen years after the two American devotees of India's BJP hosted the young apparatchik in their homes, they were now conducting a systematic campaign to boost his image and name recognition abroad. Their efforts were to prove fruitful.

By 2011, Modi was rumored to be the BJP's candidate for prime minister in the 2014 general election. His name was floated at least a year before the Supreme Court's SIT supposedly *cleared* him of guilt for the 2002 pogrom. In 2012, his backers declared the SIT's conclusion that there was "not enough evidence" to prosecute to be a "clean chit" and treated it as a green light to push the RSS *pracharak* into India's highest office.

Modi was elected in May 2014.

His election followed a three-year campaign by OFBJP operatives in America, which began with training camps in 2011, followed by tours of the US by RSS and BJP executives in 2012. In 2013, then BJP president Rajnath Singh toured the US and Modi gave three video conferences. OFBJP sent activists to India to canvass for the BJP in the state elections. Their campaign culminated in 2014, when thousands of volunteers staffed US-based phone banks, while nearly 2,000 activists — including a team of 650 led by Barai in person — traveled to India.

After floating to power on a *Modi wave* for the first time, the BJP wasted no time implementing its agenda to *saffronize* the country.

2014 witnessed joint strategy sessions between the BJP and the RSS as they sought to rewrite the history taught in the Indian school curriculum. Then controversy broke out, as RSS-affiliated groups were accused of forcibly *reconverting* hundreds of Muslims to Hinduism. Subsequently, Rajnath Singh (who had transitioned from the BJP presidency to a ministerial post) and Amit Shah (who had replaced Singh as BJP president) suggested that the country adopt a national *anti-conversion law* to criminalize religious conversion without state permission.

2015 saw the lynching of Mohammed Akhlaq, a Muslim man, who was dragged from his home at night and beaten to death on the suspicion that he had slaughtered a cow. Local BJP activists were implicated in Akhlaq's murder. This was one of the earliest and highest profile of what were to be many beef-related mob lynchings. Over the ensuing years, similar killings of Muslims and Dalits were replicated time and time again. Meanwhile, states like Maharashtra and Haryana responded by criminalizing cow slaughter — Maharashtra made even the possession of beef punishable by five years in prison, while Haryana imposed a ten-year sentence for cow slaughter.

2016 opened with the suicide of Rohith Vemula, a Dalit

PhD student at the University of Hyderabad, who took his own life after he was suspended for protesting an RSS-affiliated event. Protests over Vemula's death continued for months and even spilled over onto the international stage. In India, mass student protests bookended the arrest of Jawaharlal Nehru University student union president Kanhaiya Kumar, who was charged with sedition over the slogans allegedly used by some protestors. Kumar later claimed that the country was in the "clutches" of the RSS. As protests continued to spread, Modi expanded the central government's cabinet, stacking a third of it with members of RSS-affiliated groups, including at least a dozen *pracharaks*.

In 2017, Yogi Adityanath was appointed chief minister of Uttar Pradesh. While previously serving as a member of parliament in 2015, he had promised to install statues of Hindu deities in "every mosque." Earlier, while campaigning, he had promised to kill 100 Muslims for every Hindu killed by a Muslim. His claim to fame included organizing the *reconversion* — voluntary or otherwise — of thousands of Muslims and Christians to Hinduism. Soon after Adityanath took office, Chhattisgarh's chief minister Raman Singh called for the hanging of anyone who slaughtered a cow.

Meanwhile, dissenting voices were being stifled. "If you speak anything except for singing praises for the government, you risk your life," wrote Teltumbde that summer. "You could be easily charged under sedition or under any of the many draconian laws and sent for life imprisonment, if not hanged." The state, he concluded, "has raised jingoist nationalism above people and unleashed the Hindutva gangs to carry out its writ reminiscent of the black shirts of Mussolini and brown shirts of Hitler … For the last three years, we have seen a working prototype of what a fascist regime is like."

The truth of Teltumbde's warning was brutally demonstrated when Gauri Lankesh, a journalist known for her candid criticism of the RSS and BJP, was assassinated in Karnataka. The investigation implicated an RSS-affiliated activist. It also connected her murder to the 2015 killings of rationalists Govind Pansare and M. M. Kalburgi.

2018 began with a rally of hundreds of thousands of Dalits in Bhima Koregaon, Maharashtra. The gathering devolved into chaos as Hindu nationalist outfits launched an attack. In response, Dalits called a *bandh* (shutdown), blocking roads and railways.

The unrest, asserted attorneys Arun Ferreira and Colin Gonsalves, was the result of "three and a half years of belligerent Hindutva rule at the center and in various states, with its rabid cocktail of blatant communal polarization, increasing atrocities against Dalits, lynching of minorities, gender violence and bans on inter-community love enforced by ruling party stormtroopers, state crackdown on dietary choices, and clampdown on universities — all accompanied by a shrill pseudo-nationalist discourse that paints all dissent as anti-national." They argued that Modi's regime bore "similarities with Nazi Germany" and "more and more people are coming around to identify it as a form of fascism." Because the danger was "more long term," they warned against exaggerating the importance of the 2019 general election and urged people to instead "forge a front against fascism."

Then, in the state of Jammu and Kashmir, an eight-year-old Muslim girl was abducted, held for a week, and repeatedly gang-raped before she was murdered. When her killers were arrested, Hindu nationalist outfits staged rallies in their support. Two BJP state ministers joined one of the rallies: they later claimed that their party had instructed them to do so.

Meanwhile, unrest expanded across India as Dalits launched a *bharat bandh* (national shutdown) later that year. A teenage girl set herself on fire outside Yogi Adityanath's home to protest his administration's refusal to arrest a BJP state legislator whom she accused of rape. Eight men convicted of lynching a Muslim man for allegedly transporting beef were released from jail — and immediately escorted to the home of Jharkhand's chief minister Jayant Sinha to be honored with garlands.

There were staggered waves of arrests of prominent activists, writers and attorneys in multiple Indian states. Ferreira and Gonsalves, having warned about rising fascism, were among those taken into custody. K. Satyanarayana, a professor at a Hyderabad university, was not arrested but his home was searched. Afterwards, he reported that police had interrogated him about why he was "reading Marx" and keeping photos of civil rights icons like B. R. Ambedkar "instead of gods and goddesses."

These actions informed Teltumbde's conclusion later that year that "the country's pretensions of being the largest democracy in the world have been fast falling apart."

In 2019, Swami Aseemanand, the *pracharak* who had confessed to a string of terrorist attacks in the mid-2000s, was acquitted. Sadhvi Pragya Thakur was nominated for a seat in parliament — despite the fact that she was still facing trial for the same terrorist acts in which Aseemanand was implicated. BJP President Amit Shah sparked outrage when he referred to illegal immigrants from Bangladesh as "termites," while Adityanath accused the opposition of being "infected" by a "green virus" (a reference to

Muslims).

Also, in 2019, at the height of the Modi regime's crackdown on dissenters to date, Anand Teltumbde was arrested. Only one year previously, he had accused the government of criminalizing dissent, writing, "The message is loud and clear to all others: to not speak against the government."

Over the years since Modi first took office, countless students, teachers, activists and common people from all walks of life have been arrested — often on sedition charges — for sharing political memes and posting comments on social media variously labeled by the state as *defamatory, derogatory* or *obscene*. Some face charges for creating — or simply disseminating — pictures mocking Modi, other officials or even the RSS itself. Others are accused of nothing more than calling Modi names.

On 23 May 2019, after a month-long election process, in which the OFBJP again played an instrumental role, the BJP emerged victorious with 38.5% of the total vote.

"It's not a victory of BJP," comments Dr. Ashok Swain, professor of peace and conflict research at Uppsala University. "It's a victory of Modi and Modi's politics ... After Modi came to power in the last five years, this has been turned into a personality cult. BJP is now a one-man party." Swain describes Modi as "near to a god for a large number of his followers." The *pracharak*'s divine status, he asserts, was cemented by the Gujarat pogrom. "Modi became Modi because of the 2002 killing of 2,000 Muslims," he states. "RSS realized Modi's value to take over the leadership, to be their prime ministerial candidate, after 2002." Seventeen years after the pogrom, Swain believes this election was about electing a leader "for the majoritarian community to control the minority."

Modi's rise from obscurity was no accident. He is the result of a fifty-year project on the part of the RSS, a man who was groomed to be prime minister. He rode to victory on the backs of gangs of apparatchiks who are unmarried and completely dedicated to the party — *pracharaks* from the RSS, among whose ranks he got his own start in public life.

Modi's re-election was a referendum on fascism, lynching, and the unrestrained violence against minorities, dissidents and the marginalized which has been repeatedly perpetrated with impunity by the troops of the RSS and BJP.

The 2019 Indian general election demonstrated that democracy is about more than the simple act of voting or the peaceful transfer of power from one *regime* to another. It illustrated the truth of the words penned by Ambedkar in 1949: "It is quite possible for this newborn democracy to retain its form but give place to dictatorship in fact."

The essence of democracy is a free and open public forum that encourages, cultivates and protects discussion, debate and dissent. The electoral process is the least important part of a democracy. Without social democracy, political democracy is virtually irrelevant — in fact, even dangerous, because it legitimizes tyranny.

Ambedkar defined social democracy as "a way of life which recognizes liberty, equality and fraternity as the principles of life." He warned, "Political democracy cannot last unless there lies at the base of it social democracy." Quoting John Stuart Mill, he admonished India that maintaining democracy necessitates that the people refuse to "lay their liberties at the feet of even a great man."

His words, written the year before Modi was born, were perhaps never more prescient than today. "In politics, *bhakti* or hero-worship is a sure road to degradation and to eventual dictatorship," he declared. Modi epitomizes Ambedkar's prophecy.

Originally published by Areo [AreoMagazine.com].

… 3 …

How India's Ruling Party Mobilizes Indian-Americans to Win Elections

7 April 2019

India is having its first national election in five years.

Partisanship in India is no better than in the United States. Probably much worse. Political party choices polarize families, friends, and whole communities and every election season can be a very divisive time.

No wonder then that the US's nearly 4.5 million Indian-Americans watch India's elections with sharp eyes.

A recent episode on Indian-American Muslim comedian Hasan Minhaj's show illustrated the nature of the diaspora's interest in Indian politics. In a promo, he reveals his topic to Indian couples sitting at home. They are horrified: "Indian elections are a definite no-no."

"Democracy is for people with power, people with muscle power and money power," says one man. "It's not for you and me."

"There will be an accident," says one woman. "You will be burnt to death. Be gone."

"You cannot talk about Narendra Modi," warns another woman.

Indeed, unless it's something positive, then talking about Indian Prime Minister Modi can get people into real hot water.

Last year in India, for instance, a high school teacher was arrested for writing on Facebook that voting for Modi is like "garlanding a dog."

Talking about Modi in the US, meanwhile, is very controversial. The issue splits the Indian-American diaspora. One side believes in Modi and is devoted to advancing his vision for India. The other side believes Modi is a fascist leader with blood on his hands.

Nothing widens the divide more than the religious angle. Only about half of the Indian-American diaspora is Hindu. The other half are a diverse mix of Buddhist, Christian, Dalit, Muslim, Sikh, and so forth — or non-religious. Modi's party is a religious nationalist party and he identifies as a "*Hindutvavadi*" (supporter of Hindutva).

The ideology teaches that all Indians are Hindus and non-Hindus are foreign to India.

Beyond differences of opinion, the diaspora is also split in how it is involved in the Indian election.

Those who oppose Modi often follow elections in India with great interest, and maybe even talk or write about them, but do little beyond. Those who support Modi host organize rallies, training camps, and campaign events. While one side alleges that Modi staged a pogrom, thousands of volunteers from the other side return to India to physically canvass for his political party.

Perhaps another reason that talking about Indian elections is controversial is because the Indian diaspora's surpassing interest in the issue often slips into direct involvement — even to the point of serving as boots on the ground in India.

The opposition party, the Indian National Congress (INC), is just as guilty as Modi's party, the Bharatiya Janata Party (BJP), of attempting to organize direct involvement of Indian emigrants in Indian elections. Yet they cannot hold a candle to the success of the BJP in harnessing the diaspora. The Overseas Friends of BJP (OFBJP) provides the organizational structure underlying that success.

The OFBJP was launched in America in April 1992 to

counter negative press.

Eight months later, in December, a BJP-organized crowd of 150,000 tore down a mosque in India. Their fervor was stoked by speeches from BJP elected officials and even the party president, who demanded that the government build a Hindu temple there instead. Razing the mosque provoked nationwide riots in which an estimated 2,000 Muslims were killed. In response, the opposition-controlled central government temporarily banned the Rashtriya Swayamsevak Sangh (RSS), a paramilitary involved in the violence.

The BJP, which was created by the RSS in 1980, responded to the scandal by establishing a strong international presence of trained party activists. Internationally, the OFBJP eventually expanded to nearly 40 chapters. In America, their membership is largely composed of US citizens.

The OFBJP-US says its goal is to project a "positive and correct image of India" in the West and "correct any distortions" in media coverage. They work hand-in-glove with BJP leadership back in India. For years leading up to Modi's 2014 election, OFBJP chief Vijay Jolly toured the US to speak at diaspora rallies and meet American politicians.

"We need to touch base with as many among the diaspora as possible and to indoctrinate them with the BJP ideology," Jolly says. Speaking in 2015, after the BJP won in India, he urged the OFBJP to be "expansionist." He has since been replaced by Vijay Chauthaiwale as head of the BJP's Foreign Affairs Cell.

Considering its 2014 levels, any expansion of the OFBJP-US would make its reach and potential for influence truly colossal.

Nationwide, it boasts 18 chapters in 13 states. In 2014, it reportedly had 4,000 members. It has an elected National Executive Committee of ten people and a nearly 40-person National Council.

In 2013, over 1,000 people turned up to watch Modi deliver a live, televised address to the OFBJP-US's annual convention in Florida. When the BJP won India's state elections in December 2013, the group organized victory parties around the country. In Houston, Texas, over 300 people showed up.

Then the OFBJP-US swung into high gear.

They had a three-pronged strategy. Organize phone-banks for Indian-Americans to call back to India and tell people to vote for the BJP. Finance a Modi victory fund. Travel back to India to put boots on the ground to campaign for the BJP directly. Like a sleeper cell waiting for orders, the group sprung into action in January 2014.

In Houston alone, a diaspora media outlet reports that 700 people "worked round the clock to motivate voters in India." The key organizer was Ramesh Bhutada, who also happens to be Vice-President of the American chapter of India's RSS paramilitary. Nationwide, then OFBJP-US President Chandrakant Patel said that thousands of activists were making 200 calls or more per day.

How much money OFBJP members actually donated to Modi's victory fund is a difficult thing to determine. Yet the mass mobilization of US-based BJP backers who went to India to canvass for Modi was widely reported.

By March 2014, Chandrakant Patel was personally leading a team of over 1,000 OFBJB-US operatives. Aside from promoting the party, some of them reportedly even ran polling booths. They remained in country for the duration of the phased, month-long voting process.

Their hard work paid off. Modi was announced as the new Prime Minister on 12 May. Over the ensuing weeks, the OFBJP-US hosted victory parties throughout America. One event in Atlanta, Georgia drew a crowd of 700. Others also drew hundreds.

Because of his human rights record, Modi was barred from visiting the US in 2005. As the newly-elected executive of India, however, he was now free to travel. He soon made plans to do so.

To herald Modi's arrival, Foreign Affairs Cell head Vijay Jolly again began touring the US In September 2014, just four months after he was elected, Prime Minister Modi spoke to a crowd of nearly 20,000 in New York City. It was a publicity bonanza which enthused BJP backers all around America. For instance, diaspora media reports that Vijay Pallod, who campaigned for Modi in India, flew from Texas just to attend.

After 2014, the OFBJP-US continued to organize rallies, stage protests, and host tours by BJP elected officials from India, expand its membership, and train its activists.

The new OFBJP-US President, Krishna Reddy Anugula, estimates the group has a loose network of up to 300,000 Indian-Americans. They began mobilizing months ago in preparation for when polls open in India on 11 April 2019. Coordinated phone-banking is underway, activists are making hundreds of phone calls each, and putting in hours a day after work to support the Indian political party from America.

Anugula says that thousands of Indian American operatives will travel to India to work until the phased elections end.

While these teams permeate India, trained activists in

the US are making a stir.

In February, after a local youth bombed a military convoy in Kashmir, the BJP blamed Pakistan and began agitating for war. As tensions soared between the two nuclear-armed powers, the OFBJP organized protests in at least six US states to demand that India attack Pakistan. Signs said things such as "world hates Pakistan."

They also began hosting *Chai pe Charcha* (Chat Over Tea) events. *Chai pe Charchas* have occurred in Washington, New York, Virginia, Michigan, Texas, and many other locations. One in Chicago on 3 March featured Sunil Deodhar, a BJP national secretary.

From America, they have also heeded the call of India's Prime Minister.

Terming himself a *"chowkidar"* (watchman), Modi declared in March, "Your *chowkidar* is standing firm and serving the nation." He called on everyone working for India to say *"Main Bhi Chowkidar"* (I am a watchman). Obediently answering Modi, activists attending *Chai pe Charcha* events began publicly pledging to work for his re-election.

Most recently, at the end of March, over 400 activists gathered in California's Silicon Valley for a conference featuring Kailash Vijayvargiya, a BJP national general secretary.

Thus, the OFBJP's operational approach seems to follow this model:

Embrace the political party line. Emigrate. Take up US citizenship, which requires renouncing Indian citizenship. Spread the mother country's party line to project a "positive" image in the adopted homeland. Cultivate diaspora interest in the party. Return to India — as US citizens — to campaign for that party and instruct Indian citizens who to vote for.

Thus, every election season, the BJP harnesses the help of people who are dedicated to keeping the BJP in power in India despite having abandoned life in India themselves.

Elections in India conclude on 19 May. Until then, the OFBJP promises to grow only more heavily involved. The impact of thousands of American boots on the ground in India remains to be seen.

It appears, however, that Indian-Americans organized by the BJP have already played a huge role in influencing Indian elections and are working to expand that role.

Perhaps that influence — some might call it interference — is one reason why, as Hasan Minhaj discovered, the topic of India's 2019 General Election is no laughing matter for the Indian-American diaspora.

Originally published by The Citizen [TheCitizen.in].

— 4 —
BJP May Have Expelled Sunita Gaur, But It Has Always Rewarded Communal Violence

2 July 2019

Sunita Singh Gaur of Ramkola, Uttar Pradesh, India secured for herself a place in history when she soared to international infamy after an explicit social media summons for "Hindu brothers" to gang-rape Muslim "mothers and sisters."

The jaw-dropping demand might have attracted little attention if it were not for Gaur's role as head of the Ramkola chapter of the Mahila Morcha [women's wing] of the Bharatiya Janata Party. Even then, it likely would have been dismissed as an aberration — the freakish ramblings of some bigoted crackpot who managed to slip unvetted into a party leadership role — if it were not remarkably consistent with the actions of some of the most notorious members of her party and the Hindutva ideology upon which it was founded.

"It was a religious duty of every Muslim to kidnap, and force into their own religion, non-Muslim women," alleged V.D. Savarkar in the 1960s. Decades after he articulated Hindutva as a religious nationalist political ideology — one which undergirds the Rashtriya Swayamsevak Sangh (RSS) and the BJP — Savarkar penned a history of the Indian subcontinent which was posthumously published in English as *Six Glorious Epochs of Indian History*.

The voluminous work of questionable historical accuracy claims that Muslims (both as invaders and as rulers) systematically raped "millions" of Hindu women as part of a deliberate plan for "increasing the Muslim population with special regard to the unavoidable laws of nature." Mixing his telling of history with scathing criticism of the Hindu leaders of past ages, he accuses them of embracing "perverted religious ideas about chivalry to women" which restrained them from paying "the Muslim fair sex in the same coin."

It was, as journalist Ajaz Ashraf noted, a call to employ rape as a political weapon.

Survivors of rape who speak about their experiences invariably talk about how they wish that no one else ever has to go through such suffering. Savarkar, however, put his own words into the mouths of imagined victims.

Envisioning the "plaintive screams and pitiful lamentations of the millions of molested Hindu women which reverberated throughout the length and breadth of the country," he speculated that their souls might say: "Let those Sultans and their peers take a fright that in the event of a Hindu victory our molestation and detestable lot shall be avenged on the Muslim women. Once they are haunted with this dreadful apprehension, that the Muslim women, too, stand in the same predicament in case the Hindus win, the future Muslim conquerors will never dare to think of such molestation of Hindu women."

While employing distinctly unvarnished rhetoric in contrast to Savarkar's flowery language, Sunita Singh Gaur proposed an identical policy. "To protect India," she said in her Facebook post (which came to light in late June 2019), "Hindu brothers must barge into every Muslim home by making a group of 10 to 20, and gang-rape their women." The defilement, she insisted, must be done "openly on the streets," after which the victims should be hung "in the middle of [the] bazaar for others to see."

Gaur's post prompted swift and extensive outrage as it

was first shared across social media platforms and then widely reported by mainstream media. On 29 June, Mahila Morcha national president Vijaya Rahatkar posted on Twitter: "The lady in question has been expelled." Rahatkar offered words of assurance. "BJP Mahila Morcha will not tolerate any hateful comments whatsoever."

Yet, while the expulsion was necessary action, other recent statements — and actions — by higher-profile BJP leaders suggest that Gaur's dismissal merely means that the party is washing its hands off a low-ranking member who became a liability.

Yogi Adityanath remains one of the most prominent and egregious examples of the BJP not only turning a blind eye to poisonous rhetoric but actually promoting those who employ it. Few are more notorious — or prolific — when it comes to producing hate speech. When he was appointed chief minister of Uttar Pradesh, Amnesty International India took the exceptional step of issuing a statement directly denouncing a single politician. He must, said Amnesty, "publicly withdraw his previous inflammatory statements against Muslims and other religious minorities."

A former MP, the volatile Adityanath founded the Hindu Yuva Vahini in 2002 to, ostensibly, "promote the harmonious development of society." Allegations against the HYV's include conversions, targeted killings, incitement of riots and burning of trains.

"If I ask for blood, they will give me blood," said Adityanath in 2009. "When I ask them to rise and protect our Hindu culture, they obey."

Adityanath's idea of how to "protect Hindu culture" closely resembles Sunita Singh Gaur's idea of how to "protect India." At one rally in the mid-2000s, he argued that a religious war is imminent because Muslim and Hindu cultures cannot co-exist — then sat and listened as another speaker called on the audience to dig up Muslim women from their graves and rape them. At another rally, Adityanath dwelled on the supposed problem of Hindu girls eloping with Muslim men. In a call and response with the crowd of 1,000 or more, he declared, "If they take take one Hindu girl, we'll take 100 Muslim girls. If they kill one Hindu, there will be 100 that we kill."

Nevertheless, Adityanath was sworn-in as chief minister at a grand ceremony in 2017, attended by Prime Minister Narendra Modi and BJP president Amit Shah.

Elsewhere in India, the use of rape as a political weapon has seen instances of BJP support for the rapists. In January 2018, the abominable gang-rape of an eight-year-old girl in Jammu and Kashmir's Kathua, it emerged, was a conspiracy to terrorize the Muslims into fleeing the region. The conspiracy backfired as several people were arrested, including a local Hindu priest and multiple police officers — one of whom was accused of master-minding, others of destroying evidence.

Rather than disavowing the accused, sections of the BJP leapt to their defense. The party's state secretary, Vijay Sharma, founded the Hindu Ekta Manch for their support. When the HEM organized a February rally of more than 5,000 people, at least three BJP state legislators joined: ministers Choudhary Lal Singh and Chander Prakash Ganga as well as MLA Rajiv Jasrotia. "We went there on the party's instruction," Ganga said. In April, when the Kathua rape — and these BJP leaders' support for the rapists — made international headlines, Ganga and Singh resigned.

Meanwhile, as the Indian diaspora organized protests to support the child victim, Modi spoke out during a mid-

April visit to London. Rather than censuring the ministers, he merely noted that "rape is rape," and instructed to not "politicize rape incidents."

Two weeks later, Jasrotia was sworn-in as a state cabinet minister and assigned the same portfolio vacated by Singh. Explaining that the party did not want Singh and Ganga to step down, BJP spokesperson Ram Madhav stated, "They resigned because the media created an impression that they were supporting the rape accused."

In June, Madhav described their attendance at the rally as an "indiscretion," using the opportunity to lash out at Congress for "trying to politicize the issue."

If attending a rally to support a gang who raped a child is an "indiscretion," what does one call participation in a full-scale massacre of a minority community?

During the 2002 Gujarat riots too, attackers implemented what was essentially Sunita Singh Gaur's recommendation. "Women and girls were gang-raped in public view before being hacked and burned to death," reported Human Rights Watch. Gaur's explicit post advised rapists to "cut them and impale their vagina" — and, as HRW reported, countless eyewitnesses reported women in 2002 were "raped and cut" while one victim even arrived at a refugee camp "unconscious and with an iron rod stuck inside her vagina."

"I made bombs, rocket launchers, swords, and distributed them across Gujarat," boasted Haresh Bhatt in a video secretly filmed by *Tehelka*. Then coordinator of Bajrang Dal, Bhatt continued, "Firearms and swords were smuggled in from other states as well."

Speaking about Modi, then the chief minister of Gujarat, he said, "What he did, no chief minister has ever done.... He had given us three days.... After three days, he asked us to stop and everything came to a halt." Speaking to *The New York Times* at the conclusion of those three days, Bhatt dubbed himself "the first enemy of Muslims."

"We didn't spare any of them," local Bajrang Dal leader Babu Bajrangi told *Tehelka*. "They shouldn't be allowed to breed. Whoever they are, even if they're women or children, there's nothing to be done with them; cut them down. Thrash them, slash them, burn the bastards."

He bragged about his role in the attack on the Muslim majority Naroda Patiya neighborhood. In one of the worst massacres of the three-day pogrom, over 70 of the Naroda dead (according to official figures) were women and children. "Everyone was on a killing spree," said Bajrangi. "There were bodies everywhere." They "dumped the corpses in a well" — except for those they set on fire.

"Hacked, burnt, set on fire, many things were done," he said. "We believe in setting them on fire because these bastards say they don't want to be cremated." Praising Modi for doing what "nobody can do," he declared, "It was his hand all the way."

At the end of the day, he said, "I came back after I killed them them, called up the home minister, and went to sleep." The home minister then was Gordhan Zadafia. In charge of state security forces then, he is a long-time VHP activist turned BJP politician.

"I spoke to Gordhan Zadafia," said Bajrangi. "He told me to leave Gujarat and go into hiding."

One of the participants who didn't go into hiding was BJP MLA Maya Kodnani, despite partnering with Bajrangi as a key leader of the Naroda Patiya massacre. Eyewitnesses repeatedly identified both of them, testifying that they distributed weapons and urged on the attackers. "Mayaben was moving around all day in an open jeep,"

Suresh Richard, one of those attackers, told *Tehelka*. "She was saying, 'Jai Shri Ram. Jai Shri Ram.' … She kept raising slogans. She said, carry on with your work."

What was Richard's work? "When thousands of hungry men go in, they will eat some fruit or the other," he said. "Many Muslim girls were being killed and burnt to death anyway, some people must have helped themselves to the fruit. The fruit was there so it had to be eaten. I also ate…. That scrap-dealer's girl, Naseemo…. I got on top…. Then I pulped her." Afterwards, he said, he "had to go killing again."

Although Vijaya Rahatkar claims it has expelled Sunita Singh Gaur because the BJP Mahila Morcha "will not tolerate any hateful comments whatsoever," participation in the wholesale slaughter of men, women, and children was not enough to convince the BJP to expel MLA Kodnani. She was later made Minister of State for Women and Child Development. Haresh Bhatt, meanwhile, was rewarded with a seat in the state legislature.

"Clearly, it was the Hindutva card that worked in our favor," said Bhatt when he won in December 2002. "This election was fought for establishing a Hindu nation."

Bhatt was never charged. Kodnani and Bajrangi were finally charged, however. Their trial began in 2009. In 2012, ten years after the pogrom, both were convicted and sentenced — Kodnani to 28 years and Bajrangi to life. Yet Modi — who allegedly did what "no chief minister has ever done" — never faced any legal repercussions.

In 2010, while the Supreme Court was investigating the pogrom, there was talk that Zadafia might testify against Modi. That idea died as *Times of India* reported that RSS executives were contacting Zadafia to "persuade him not to take this step at this juncture." Then, in 2012, the court's investigating team concluded that there was not enough prosecutable evidence to charge Modi. That cleared the path for him to campaign for the prime ministership. Then in April 2018, a Gujarat court acquitted Kodnani. In March 2019, the Supreme Court determined that Bajrangi was "in bad shape" and should be granted bail.

For his loyalty and silence, Zadafia was entrusted with managing the BJP's campaign in Uttar Pradesh during the 2019 Lok Sabha polls. It was a cathartic release for a man who once was considered likely to turn state's evidence against Modi. It was also an affirmation of his ideological commitment. Upon announcement of his appointment, *The Economic Times* reported, "What is, however, unquestionable is the 64-year-old leader's Hindutva credentials as his ties with RSS and VHP always remained strong."

Zadafia's efforts paid off. The BJP swept the parliamentary elections in Uttar Pradesh. "Earlier it was a Modi wave," he told *The Week*. "This time, it is a Modi tsunami across India."

On 28 May, just a few days after the results of that "tsunami" were announced, Modi posted a video on Twitter. Set to a melodramatic musical score, the video shows him paying obeisance to a photo of Savarkar, declaring:

We bow to Veer Savarkar on his *Jayanti* [birthday].

Veer Savarkar epitomizes courage, patriotism and unflinching commitment to a strong India.

He inspired many people to devote themselves towards nation building.

It was not Modi's first time eulogizing the father of

Hindutva. "Savarkar ji's personality was full of special qualities," he said in 2014. "He was also a striking poet and a social reformer who always emphasized on goodwill and unity." He added: "We remember and salute Veer Savarkar's tireless efforts towards the regeneration of our Motherland."

Yet what was it that Savarkar so poetically emphasized as necessary for regeneration of the motherland? "Were a serpent (an inveterate national enemy) to come with a view to bite the motherland, he should be smashed to pieces with a surprise attack, deceit, or cunning or in any other way possible," he wrote in *Six Glorious Epochs*. Accusing Muslims of "slaughtering Hindus irrespective of their age or sex and pulling down the Hindu holy places of worship," he declared: "Because the Hindus did not emulate the Muslims in this respect, these local Muslims who were left alive and unmolested, turned traitors, like serpents fed and fostered as pets."

"A serpent, whether male or female, if it comes to bite must be killed," he asserted. Arguing that "the whole of the Hindu nation" was, during times of Muslim rule, "utterly infatuated with the perverted sense of virtues," he specified one of those virtues as "the suicidal Hindu idea of chivalry to women."

The problem, he insisted, was that "only Muslim men, and not women, were taken prisoner" and that "even when they were taken prisoner in battles, the Muslim women — royal ladies as also the commonest slaves — were invariably sent back safe and sound to their respective families."

He was horrified that "this act was glorified by the Hindus as their chivalry towards the enemy women and the generosity of their religion."

Such chivalry must be rejected as a vice rather than a virtue — so thought Savarkar.

Sunita Singh Gaur seems to have thought the same. Her despicable comments are inexcusable, yet she may certainly be excused for mistakenly believing that she could get away with expressing such views as a BJP leader. Many other party leaders have succeeded in actually enacting rather than merely expressing the extent of violence Gaur recommended. Perhaps the simple truth is that she lacked the social capital necessary to receive the party's protection — even reward — for what she did.

She lacked the political power of an Adityanath, a Kodnani, or a Modi.

One thing is certain. Expelling Gaur is not a panacea for the hatred which the BJP has not only tolerated but given safe haven, fostered, and purveyed throughout the country. The very first step on a sincere journey towards eradicating "hateful comments" — and the horrifying atrocities they produce — would be the rejection of Savarkar and his poisonous ideology of Hindutva.

Originally published by The Wire [TheWire.in].

— 5 —
Cultural Malware: The Rise of India's RSS

12 March 2020

In 2019, on Christmas Day, the Rashtriya Swayamsevak Sangh (RSS) marched through the streets of the Indian city of Hyderabad in the state of Telangana. Armed with lathis — the iron-bound bamboo poles used by police — the uniformed cadres of the RSS paraded to the beating of drums and blaring of bugles. The march followed a 3-day training camp to increase Telangana's nearly 3,500 RSS *shakhas* (branches). At least 8,000 *swayamsevaks* (members) were expected to participate, reported *The Indian Express*.

It was a grand display of incredible discipline and military precision that, for some, conjured up images of another organization. "RSS today took a massive Nazi-style march," wrote Ashok Swain, a professor of Peace and Conflict Studies at Uppsala University in Sweden. Claiming that the RSS was "inspired by the Nazis," poet Meera Kandasamy wrote: "Their military style uniform, marching… the way they go after one enemy is all in line with the fascists."

The march also drew criticism for another reason: all other rallies in the city were banned at the time. Hyderabad's population is 30% Muslim, more than twice the national average. It has been a stronghold for rallies against the newly passed Citizenship Amendment Act (CAA) and the proposed National Register of Citizens (NRC). Yet, seeking to quash dissent, the Government had specifically prohibited public assemblies — the only exception made was for the Hindu nationalist paramilitary, the RSS.

The RSS is probably the world's oldest and largest paramilitary group. A secretive, unregistered organization, its size is unknown, but estimated at approximately six million *swayamsevaks*. It keeps no records and has no bank accounts. It is uniformed, armed, and all-male. Women are only allowed in the separate women's wing. It also has countless special-purpose subsidiary organizations, the most important of which are:

• Akhil Bhartiya Vidyarthi Parishad (ABVP), the student wing, founded in 1949.

• Vishwa Hindu Parishad (VHP), the religious wing, founded in 1964.

• Bharatiya Janata Party (BJP), the political wing, founded in 1980.

• Bajrang Dal, the VHP's youth wing, founded in 1984.

These groups maintain "symbiotic links" with the RSS, write historians Walter Andersen and Shridhar Damle, by recruiting *swayamsevaks* "who have already demonstrated organizational skills in the RSS," a process which guarantees a "high degree of conformity" in behavioral norms and a "high degree of loyalty" to the mother organization. According to MS Golwalkar, the RSS's second and longest serving Supreme Leader (1940-1973), the mission of these affiliates was to serve "their own specific roles in their respective fields," while also working as "recruiting centers for the Sangh from the ideological point of view." He ordered them to "ideologically capture all other fields." Their common ideology is Hindutva.

The US Commission on International Religious Freedom calls Hindutva an ideology "which holds non-Hindus as foreign to India." Amnesty International says: "Hindutva is the political ideology of an exclusively Hindu nation." An exclusively Hindu nation is exactly what the current Supreme Leader of the RSS, Mohan Bhagwat, insists that India is and should be. One of the many times Bhagwat reiterated this demand was in October 2019, at an event celebrating the foundation of RSS. "The vision and proclamation of the Sangh regarding the identity of the nation, social identity of all of us, and the identity of the country's nature are clear, well-thought-of and firm that [India] is Hindustan, [a] Hindu [nation]," he declared.

He also said: "I was the RSS chief in 2009 as well, but not so many people were here to listen to me. Today, there are more people, because of the growth of the RSS in various sectors."

Indeed, the RSS has grown — or, rather, metastasized.

The RSS hoped to become "the core around which society itself would become strengthened and cohesive," explains journalist Hartosh Singh Bal. It was intended to provide a foundation for the country by becoming a predominant group with a hand in every aspect of life in India. Under Bhagwat's leadership, today the RSS operates as a state within a state. It is essentially, a shadow government. It is more than just that, argues novelist Arundhati Roy. "No longer a shadow state or a parallel state, it is the state," she writes. "Day by day, we see examples of its control over the media, the police, the intelligence agencies. Worryingly, it appears to exercise considerable influence over the armed forces, too."

It has taken decades of quiet, hard work for the RSS to achieve this level of social and political control. For a long time, the paramilitary was busy laboring at the state level. In 2002, for instance, Roy reported that "the police, the administration and the political cadres at every level" had been "systematically penetrated" in the state of Gujarat.

This is where Modi first cut his teeth as a BJP politician. It is also where the RSS conducted its first pogrom of the 21st Century, which the former leader of the VHP called a "successful experiment which will be repeated all over the country."

"The traditional muscle power of the BJP has always been the RSS," said a former US ambassador to India. "The RSS can survive without the BJP but the BJP cannot exist without the RSS. This inextricably links the BJP to the RSS's Hindutva (Hindu nationalist) agenda. If the BJP does not toot the Hindutva horn, the RSS will not mobilize the Hindu voters."

Today, however, the RSS's role is much broader than merely mobilizing voters. It doesn't just provide boots on the ground to help win elections — it pulls the strings of the party's elected officials. Indian attorney AG Noorani calls the BJP "a creature of the RSS," adding: "Without it the BJP will collapse. Not only does the RSS provide the muscle, cadres who constitute the indispensable foot soldiers during elections, but also the top officials."

The background of the country's leadership clearly reflects this. In 2014, when Modi first took office as Prime Minister, 41 members of his government's 66-person cabinet had an RSS background. Before reshuffling the cabinet in 2017, the BJP first held a "crucial coordination meeting" with the RSS. Today, 38 out of 53 ministers — nearly 75 percent — hail from the RSS. That includes the infamous duo of Prime Minister Narendra Modi and Home Minister Amit Shah. The two met in 1982, when Modi was 31 and Shah was 17; they became inseparable partners and rose to power through the labors of the RSS. Shah, who is now president of the BJP, acts as Modi's lieutenant and probable successor. Other cabinet members with an RSS background include: Defense Minister Rajnath Singh; Transportation Minister Nitin Gadkari; Human Resource Development Minister Ramesh Pokhriyal (who is in charge of education); and Ravi Shankar Prasad, who is Minister of both Communications as well as Law and Justice.

With so much power in its hands, criticism of the paramilitary has become nearly an anti-national act of sedition. "Any form of dissent, or attempt to question the views of the RSS, the BJP or Prime Minister Narendra Modi, is now framed as a threat to national integrity," writes Hartosh Singh Bal. "In effect, the idea of the nation has come to be conflated with an ideology, a political party or an individual."

At the core of the RSS's ideology is the idea that only Hindus hold a birthright to India, and so the country should be a Hindu *Rashtra* (nation). Technically, the group today teaches that a Hindu *Rashtra* is not something to work towards so much as it is merely a given fact of reality. They believe that India is already a Hindu nation. One RSS ideologue recently argued, for instance, that Hindutva "is an adjective of the nation, not an objective," stating: "Hindu nation is an appropriate adjective in geo-cultural context."

Nevertheless, since the Republic of India is officially a secular democracy, securing the foundations of what they believe is already a Hindu nation does require legislative and judicial action. "When the BJP came to power in 2014, its Hindu chauvinism was kept on a short leash," writes journalist Kenan Malik. However, "a resounding second victory" gave Modi "license to pursue exclusionary policies without restraint." Since May 2019, Modi's regime has moved with blitzkrieg speed to implement the RSS's platform. All of the BJP's highest profile and most controversial actions since then are key items on the RSS agenda:

- Revoking Article 370 of the Indian Constitution, thus scrapping the Muslim-majority State of Jammu and Kashmir of its semi-autonomous status.
- Giving a green light to build Ram Mandir — a Hindu temple — on disputed land in the city of Ayodhya in the state of Uttar Pradesh.
- Passing the Citizenship Amendment Act, which makes religion the basis for acquiring Indian citizenship.
- And proposing a National Register of Citizens, which would require every Indian resident to prove their citizenship.

In Uttar Pradesh, where around 20 people died in just the first few days of protests, the BJP Chief Minister Yogi Adityanath vowed to "take revenge" on protestors. His vow of "revenge" manifested in targeted violence against Muslims throughout the state.Following the adoption of the CAA in December 2019, the streets of India were engulfed by mass protests demanding its repeal and opposing introduction of the NRC. These are, essentially, protests against the implementation of the RSS's agenda. Protestors faced vicious suppression. Nearly 70 have died. Countless videos show masses of peaceful protestors breaking like waves on the rocks as Police charge them and begin randomly brutalizing people. In Uttar Pradesh, where around 20 people died in just the first few days of protests, the BJP Chief Minister Yogi Adityanath vowed to "take revenge" on protestors. His vow of "revenge" manifested in targeted violence against Muslims throughout the state.

Adityanath's police are accused of conducting military-style crackdowns in Muslim neighborhoods "with police opening fire on civilians, beating children, barging into homes and vandalizing property." In the midnight hours, they appeared at Muslim homes to threaten women and children unless they disclose the location of the male members of the family. There are documented reports that Muslim teenagers are being picked up by police and subjected to emotional, psychological, and physical torture for hours or days on end — and, in one incident, a 73-year-old Muslim attorney was arrested, taken to the police station, and beaten in custody while officers threatened to destroy his family, throw them all in jail to "rot for life," and rape his mother.

Throughout India, the Police are brutalizing protestors. When violence erupted in Delhi in late February 2020, the Police were accused of breaking down the doors of Muslim homes and dragging the occupants out to hand them over to mobs. They were filmed beating a pile of bloodied young Muslim men while forcing them to sing the national anthem. One of the victims later died. In another instance, a man who joined the mob-stoning of Muslims claims that they were running out of stones, so "the police brought some and told us to throw them."

It was the worst communal violence to hit Delhi since the 1984 Sikh Genocide and, over just a few days, well over 50 — mostly Muslims — died in what journalist Mira Kamdar calls a pogrom. "Mobs targeting a single religious group were allowed to run riot, unchecked by police," writes Kamdar. "That is the definition of a pogrom."

As this Hindu nationalist mob, aided and abetted by the Police and originally instigated by a BJP politician, dominated the streets, their violence was widely blamed on the RSS which, as seen in Hyderabad on Christmas Day, has perfected the art of dominating the streets.

Violence is the inevitable result of the RSS's

domination of the streets. Over the past few decades, the international community has increasingly acknowledged this. The United Nations has warned about the militancy of "Hindu extremists" who are attracted to "ultra-nationalism," engage in "political exploitation of religion," and perpetrate violence against Christians and Muslims. Amnesty International and Human Rights Watch have both warned that escalating violence against religious minorities is carried out by the RSS and its subsidiaries. The US State Department has described the RSS as an "extremist" group, warning that the Sangh has been "implicated in incidents of violence and discrimination against Christians and Muslims" — and, in 2018, the Central Intelligence Agency categorized the VHP and Bajrang Dal as "militant religious organizations."

The kind of violence in which the RSS — and the Hindu nationalist movement it has cultivated — is implicated includes assassinations, bombings, and even pogroms against Christians, Muslims, and anyone who stands up against its xenophobic agenda.

In 2017, for example, journalist Gauri Lankesh was cut down by the bullets of a Hindu nationalist assassin who was later arrested, gave a confession, and was linked to the murder of two other anti-RSS intellectuals. As someone known for allegedly calling the RSS "a multi-hooded poisonous snake," Lankesh anticipated the risk of assassination. A year before her death, she said: "We are living in such times that Modi [devotees] and the Hindutva brigade welcome the killings… and celebrate the deaths… of those who oppose their ideology, their political party and their supreme leader Narendra Modi…. Let me assure you, they are keen to somehow shut me up too."

Terrorist bombings also figure into the RSS's portfolio

of violence. From 2006 to 2008, for instance, a wave of bombings hit Muslim targets throughout India, killing hundreds in the States of Haryana, Maharashtra, Rajasthan and Telangana. One of the worst incidents was the bombing of the Samjhauta Express, the "friendship train" running between India and Pakistan. Seventy people died. The investigation into the attacks implicated, among others, a full-time RSS worker named Swami Aseemanand who, in interviews with media, claimed that the violence was directly sanctioned by the RSS Chief Mohan Bhagwat. Aseemanand said Bhagwat agreed that it was necessary to "do some violence in the name of Hindus," but instructed him: "Don't link it to the Sangh…. If you do it, then people won't say that we committed a crime for the sake of committing a crime. It will be connected to the ideology. This is very important for the Hindus. Please do this. You have our blessings."

Anti-minority pogroms are one of the RSS's most tried and trusted tactics; in fact, it's linked to over a dozen such massacres. By 1947, the RSS had penetrated every major area of the subcontinent and boasted up to a half a million members. The British were leaving, the subcontinent was being partitioned, and the Maharajah of Jammu and Kashmir was faced with the choice to join Pakistan or India or remain independent. As he wavered, the chief of the RSS visited to pressure him to join India. His visit followed the launch of a state-sanctioned pogrom in which the Maharajah's troops joined hands with the RSS to slaughter Muslims of Jammu. By the end, the total number of people killed was catastrophically high. Lowball estimates place the death toll at 20,000. In 1948, though, *The Times of London* claimed that "237,000 Muslims were systematically exterminated."

In 1969, Gujarat was struck by "the worst communal riots the country had seen since Partition." A few months after the RSS held a three-day rally in Gujarat where its chief pleaded for a "Hindu Nation," sword-wielding mobs of people from the RSS and other Hindu nationalist groups attacked Muslims throughout the state. Officially, over 400 died; unofficially, the death toll ran as high as 2,000.

The next two decades brought a series of massacres. From 1970 to 1989, riots in Bihar, Gujarat, Maharashtra, and Uttar Pradesh left thousands of Muslims dead. The RSS persistently protested its complete innocence, but witnesses and investigations all implicated the paramilitary and its subsidiaries.

Finally, however, the RSS played its hand openly.

The Babri mosque had stood in the city of Ayodhya since the early 1500s. In the mid-1980s, however, the VHP launched a campaign to reclaim the ground on which the mosque stood, alleging that it is the location where the Hindu deity Ram was born. Soon, the BJP formally joined the campaign, with party president LK Advani leading the charge. In December 1992, hundreds of thousands rallied around the mosque to listen to speeches by Advani and other BJP leaders. Sparked by their fiery rhetoric, the mob surged forward and began demolishing the mosque. Then came the pogroms. Anti-Muslim violence spread throughout northern India and lasted into the new year. The death toll was up to 3,000. None of the violence was spontaneous. According to a UN investigation, the Sangh "infiltrated the crowd," planned the mosque's destruction, and "brought about the death of Muslim demonstrators... [and] the pillage of Muslim houses and shops," and the widespread violence that followed. The Indian government responded by briefly banning the RSS, VHP, and Bajrang

Dal but, by 1998, the BJP rose to national power for the first time with Advani as Deputy Prime Minister.

The BJP still held national power when Modi was elected as chief minister of Gujarat in February 2002. Three days later, the State was engulfed in a carnage. A train burned, killing 59 Hindu pilgrims returning from Ayodhya. Modi immediately declared it an act of terrorism and blamed it on Pakistan. His government then transported the charred bodies to the state's capital and handed them over to the VHP. They declared a statewide bandh (shutdown). Then blood began to flow. For three days, mobs ran rampage across Gujarat. Over a dozen cities witnessed major incidents of violence. By the end, up to 2,000 (or more) Muslims lay dead. Eyewitnesses claim attackers were armed with voter lists naming Muslim targets. Some of the mobs were even led by BJP state legislators who distributed weapons and issued orders. Survivors say that, when they appealed to police for help, they were sometimes told: "We have no orders to save you." Witnesses claim police even fired on victims.

Soon after the violence ended, a BJP state minister (and RSS member) blew the whistle. He told media that he — along with other State and Police officials — was summoned to a meeting at Modi's home on the night the pogrom began. They were ordered to stand down so that the mobs could "vent their frustration." A senior police officer later corroborated the claim and then a sting by an Indian magazine caught multiple leaders from the RSS, VHP, and BJP bragging about their participation in the pogrom and boasting that Modi had given them three days to do whatever they wanted.

One of the most recent anti-minority pogroms occurred in 2008. When a VHP leader was murdered in Odisha, the group blamed the local Christian community. Mobs led by a BJP state legislator began attacking Christian homes, churches, and even orphanages. Around 100 or more Christians were left dead and tens of thousands were displaced to relief camps. Later, Odisha's chief minister bluntly stated: "Members of RSS, VHP, and Bajrang Dal were involved in the violence."

It's no surprise that the RSS is responsible for such shocking violence considering its ideological ties to European fascism.

In 2011, in Norway, white supremacist terrorist Anders Breivik slaughtered 77 people. Breivik's lengthy manifesto details how he was inspired by other extremist and nationalist groups around the globe. Pointing to the RSS, he praised them for how they "dominate the streets" and "often riot and attack Muslims... usually after the Muslims disrespect and degrade Hinduism too much." He admired the RSS so much — saying that "our goals are more or less identical" — that he called for collaboration with them, writing: "It is essential that [... we] learn from each other and cooperate as much as possible."

Breivik's admiration for the RSS is quite natural considering that the correlation between fascism in the West and Hindu nationalism in the East traces all the way back to the paramilitary's origins in the 1920s.

The religious nationalist political ideology of Hindutva was first articulated by VD Savarkar, whose brother was one of the five people who co-founded the RSS. Another co-founder was BS Moonje. He was the mentor of yet another co-founder, KB Hedgewar, who became the paramilitary's first Supreme Leader. All three — Savarkar, Moonje, and Hedgewar — were also leaders in the Hindu Mahasabha, a religious nationalist political party formed in

1915. They embraced the idea that, to quote Bal, the subcontinent "had seen a steady decline from a glorious Hindu past." Convinced that losing touch with this past made Hindus "easy prey to foreign invaders, whether they were the Muslims or the British," these men committed themselves to "reviving this ancient past."

In doing so, they advanced the idea that being Indian meant being Hindu. Thus, anything or anyone that was non-Hindu represented the subjugation and oppression of Hindus. True freedom for the Hindu people could only be achieved by recognizing the subcontinent for what it had always been since time immemorial: a Hindu nation. As these three men cultivated the Hindu nationalist movement in India, they took ideological inspiration from — and even engaged in direct contact with — the rising Fascist movements in Italy and Germany.

Events moved rapidly in the 1920s and 1930s. In 1921, the year after the Nazi Party was founded, Adolf Hitler became its leader. That same year, in Italy, Benito Mussolini founded the National Fascist Party. In 1922, Mussolini led a largely successful coup in Rome. The following year, Hitler led an unsuccessful coup in Munich, was sent to prison, and began writing *Mein Kampf*. That same year, Savarkar published his manifesto, Hindutva, in which he was determined to redefine "Hindus" not as a religious community but as an ethno-nationalist one — a "Hindu Race."

Calling for the Indian subcontinent to be turned into an ethno-state of Hindus — for Hindus, and only for Hindus — he laid out a vision for unifying the "Hindu Race." India must never "lose the strength born of national and racial cohesion," he wrote. The Hindu people must be "fused and welded into an indivisible whole, till our race gets consolidated and strong sharp as steel." Insisting that "common blood" is the essence of nationality, he wrote: "We, Hindus, are all one and a nation because, chiefly, of our common blood."

Two years later, in 1925, Hitler published *Mein Kampf*, in which he declared: "What makes a people or, to be more correct, a race, is not language but blood.... Common blood belongs in a common Reich." Obsessed with protecting Germany's national and racial cohesion, he set out to fuse and weld the German people into an indivisible whole strong sharp as steel. In April 1925, Hitler founded the Schutzstaffel (Protection Squadron) — or SS — to protect the racial purity of a Germany of Germans; in September 1925, in India, Hedgewar and his cohorts founded the Rashtriya Swayamsevak Sangh (National Volunteer Organization) — or RSS.

Hedgewar insisted that the subcontinent should be called "Hindustan." Calling it "a nation of Hindu people," he compared it to a "Germany of Germans." The goal of the Sangh, he said, was "to put in[to] reality the words 'Hindustan of Hindus.'" Claiming that "the Hindu culture is the life-breath of Hindustan," he argued that the only way to protect "Hindustan" was to "first nourish the Hindu culture." If the Hindu culture "perishes" and "the Hindu society ceases to exist" in "Hindustan," he warned, it would no longer be a nation but a "mere geographical lump." He was convinced there was a grave risk of that happening. Warning that the "Hindu society" faced "daily onslaughts by outsiders," he said the only solution was to "organize the entire Hindu society." The "true path" to "national salvation" was "none other than organization," he said. "The Hindu race can save itself only through such organization.... It is to fulfill this duty of protecting the

Hindu society that the Rashtriya Swayamsevak Sangh has come into existence," declared Hedgewar.

This "protection squadron" set out to instill in the youth of India the idea that, as Golwalkar later wrote, "To offer one's all, even his dearest possessions, at the altar of [the] motherland is the first and foremost duty of every son of this soil." From the start, the paramilitary pursued youth to swell its ranks, a pattern that has continued throughout the decades. Shah and Advani, for instance, both joined at the age of 14. Modi, for his part, joined when he was eight. "The Sangh's early recruits were schoolchildren between the ages of 12 and 15," writes Hartosh Singh Bal. "When the time came for them to go to college, Hedgewar encouraged them to study outside Nagpur and expand the reach of the RSS. The training imparted at the *shakhas* reflected the needs of the young recruits Hedgewar first attracted, but its thrust remained unchanged even when the age of recruits increased."

One of those young recruits was Golwalkar, who was in his early 20s and fresh out of university when he joined the RSS's original *shakha* in Nagpur in the early 1930s. By then, the Nazis had become the second-largest political party in Germany while Mussolini — known as "*Il Duce*" — had been ruling Italy as its dictator for a decade. Impressed by reports about the Italian fascist institutions, Hedgewar's mentor, Moonje, looked to the West for inspiration. In 1931, Moonje concluded a lengthy tour of fascist Italy by meeting *Il Duce*. Applauding "the idea of fascism" for bringing out the "conception of unity amongst people," he told Mussolini that he was "much impressed" with the Italian fascist groups, had "no hesitation" to raise his voice "from the public platform" in praise of them, and concluded: "Every aspiring and growing nation needs such organizations. India needs them most for her military regeneration."

Having witnessed "their activities with my own eyes in all details," he commended how Italian fascist organizations had fostered "the military regeneration of Italy" and resolved that "India and particularly Hindu India need[s] some such institution for the military regeneration of the Hindus." He believed, however, that such an institution already existed. Noting that "our institution of Rashtriya Swayamsevak Sangh of Nagpur under Dr. Hedgewar is of this kind," Moonje pledged to spend the rest of his life "in developing and extending" it.

Upon returning to India, he argued that Hindu nationalist leaders there "should imitate the Youth movement of Germany and the... Fascist organizations of Italy," stating: "They are eminently suited for introduction in India, adapting them to suit the special conditions." Two years later, in 1933, the Nazis came to power in Germany, Hitler was made dictator, and the first concentration camp was constructed.

Meanwhile, in India, Golwalkar was appointed secretary of the Nagpur *shakha* and assigned management of the RSS's Officers' Training Camp, the institution responsible for producing *pracharaks* — the full-time workers who form the backbone of the paramilitary. The fledgling organization had already attracted the attention of the occupying British Empire, whose intelligence services warned that "the Sangh hopes to be in future India what the 'Fascisti' are to Italy and the 'Nazis' to Germany." Moonje's remarks continued to reinforce that conclusion. In a meeting with Hedgewar, he proposed that the subcontinent needed "a Hindu as a Dictator like... Mussolini or Hitler of the present day in Italy and

Germany."

In Germany, meanwhile, Hitler's dictatorship adopted the Nuremberg Laws, which required citizens to possess "German blood" and stripped Jews and others of their citizenship. The political persecution of Jews quickly shifted to physical violence. In 1938, the first Nazi pogrom against the Jews — known as *Kristallnacht*, or "Night of Broken Glass" — left nearly 100 dead as tens of thousands of Jews were shipped off to concentration camps. Yet, as the Nazis laid the foundations for the Holocaust, Savarkar argued that his concept of a Hindu nation was justified by the predominance of the racial majority in Nazi Germany.

"A Nation is formed by a majority living therein," he said less than a month before *Kristallnacht*. "What did the Jews do in Germany? They being in [a] minority were driven out." He further claimed that Indian Muslims — "like Jews in Germany" — were unlikely to assimilate into national life because they allegedly identified "themselves and their interests" more "with Muslims outside India than Hindus who live next door." He concluded, "If we Hindus in India grow stronger, in time these Muslim[s]… will have to play the part of German-Jews."

In March 1939, after the Nazis annexed Austria and as they prepared to occupy Czechoslovakia, the Hindu nationalist movement explicitly praised Hitler's embrace of Aryanism. The Hindu Mahasabha, with Savarkar as its president, declared: "Germany's solemn idea of the revival of the Aryan culture, the glorification of the Swastika, her patronage of Vedic learning and the ardent championship of the tradition of Indo-Germanic civilization are welcomed by the religious and sensible Hindus of India with a jubilant hope…. Germany's crusade against the enemies of Aryan culture will bring all the Aryan nations of the World to their senses and awaken the Indian Hindus for the restoration of their lost glory."

Seven months later, just weeks after the Second World War began with the Nazi invasion of Poland in September 1939, Moonje complained that "the Muslims are making themselves a nuisance." He claimed that "we shall have to fight" them and suggested that "the RSS may be useful and handy" for that purpose. Meanwhile, Golwalkar had been appointed second-in-command of the RSS. His ideological influence within the group expanded alongside his authority over it. That year, he published his manifesto, *We or Our Nationhood Defined*, as what Andersen and Damle call the "first systematic statement of RSS ideology."

Today, Golwalkar is revered as the Guru of the RSS. In Narendra Modi's words: "Till the end of his life, from 1940 to 1973, traveling all over India constantly, Guruji threw himself into his work of expanding the RSS." Like the other founding fathers of the Hindu nationalist movement, the Guru of the RSS explicitly praised the European fascist movements. Golwalkar extolled Mussolini's Italy for awakening "the old Roman Race consciousness of conquering the whole territory round the Mediterranean Sea" and celebrated how "the ancient Race Spirit, which prompted the Germanic tribes to over-run the whole of Europe, has re-risen in modern Germany with the result that the Nation perforce follows aspirations, predetermined by the traditions left by its depredatory ancestors." And added: "Even so with us: our Race spirit has once again roused itself….The Race Spirit has been awakening. The world has to see the might of the regenerated Hindu Nation strike down the enemy's hosts with its mighty arm…. Race Spirit calls. National consciousness blazes forth and we Hindus rally to the Hindu Standard, the *Bhagwa Dhwaj* [saffron flag], set our teeth in grim determination to wipe out the opposing forces."

He believed that European fascists had demonstrated the right to define nationality by race and proved how "every Race" possesses the "indisputable right of excommunicating from its Nationality" all who have "turned traitors" by entertaining aspirations different from those of the "National Race." Defining the "National Race" as the "Hindu Race," he declared: "Only the Hindu has been living here as the child of this soil." In other words, only Hindus held a birthright to the land. The country could only thrive, he thought, by advancing a doctrine of racial exclusivity. "In Hindustan, the land of the Hindus, lives and should live the Hindu nation," he wrote. In his mind, all non-Hindus faced only two options: "Either to merge themselves in the national race and adopt its culture, or to live at its mercy so long as the national race may allow them to do so and to quit the country at the sweet will of the national race."

Converts away from Hinduism, he insisted, had abandoned "the spirit of love and devotion for the nation" and succumbed to "divided loyalty" in place of "undivided and absolute loyalty to the nation." Conversion was, he claimed, "not merely a case of change of faith, but a change even in national identity." He declared that the only "nationalist patriots" are those who aspire to "glorify the Hindu race and Nation" — all others were "traitors" who had joined "the camp of the enemy" and left their "mother-nation in the lurch."

He claimed that non-Hindus like Christians and Muslims were "internal threats." Describing them as members of "foreign races," he demanded that they "give up their present foreign mental complexion and merge in the common stream of our national life." Claiming that they should be stripped of citizenship if they refused to be fused into "the Hindu way of life," he wrote: "The foreign races in Hindustan must either adopt the Hindu culture and language, must learn to respect and hold in reverence Hindu religion, must entertain no idea[s] but those of the glorification of the Hindu race and culture... and must lose their separate existence to merge in[to] the Hindu race, or may stay in the country, wholly subordinated to the Hindu Nation, claiming nothing, deserving no privileges, far less any preferential treatment — not even citizen's rights."

Ultimately, however, Golwalkar implied that violence may be the necessary final solution to the problem of non-Hindus residing in India. Denouncing Judaism as "an intolerant faith," he wrote: "To keep up the purity of the race and its culture, Germany shocked the world by her purging the country of the Semitic races — the Jews. Race pride at its highest has been manifested here." He concluded that Germany had set a good example by showing how it was supposedly "impossible" for different "races and cultures" to be "assimilated into one united whole." Thus, he proclaimed that the Nazi policy towards the Jews was "a good lesson for us in Hindustan to learn and profit by."

"By the time of Golwalkar's death, in 1973, the Sangh Parivar as we know it today was essentially in place," writes Bal. Not only does his ideology continue to undergird the RSS, but his visage overlooks the paramilitary's rallies. When the group paraded through the streets of Hyderabad in December 2019, Golwalkar's garlanded picture was mounted on jeeps escorted by the endless ranks of uniformed *swayamsevaks*.

The current chief of the RSS, Mohan Bhagwat, grew up

in a family of RSS activists. His father was a "close associate" of both Hedgewar and Golwalkar. He himself became a *pracharak* just two years after Golwalkar's death. Prime Minister Modi, for his part, joined the RSS in the 1950s and became a *pracharak* in 1971 under Golwalkar's leadership. Countless others who head the modern Hindu nationalist movement were also raised, proverbially, at Golwalkar's feet.

In today's information age, however, the RSS is much more cautious about how it publicly articulates its ideology. The paramilitary's leadership has repeatedly shifted its official stance about its guru's writings. Thus, in 2006, the RSS formally disowned *We or Our Nationhood Defined*, claiming it did not represent "the views of the grown Guruji nor of the RSS." Yet as early as the 1950s, scholars referred to it as the Sangh's "Bible" and, in the 1970s, senior RSS leaders said it was written to give a "scientific base" to demands for a Hindu nation. The disavowal appeared to be nothing more than image management. The book was so "brutally candid," argues Noorani, that "a desperate attempt was made by the RSS to distance itself from it."

The disavowal was accompanied by a reaffirmation of Golwalkar's second book, *Bunch of Thoughts*, which he published in 1966. Yet that book mirrors the xenophobic rhetoric of *We*, the only major difference being that — in light of historical circumstances — Golwalkar omitted the overt praise of European fascism. In 2018, the RSS again altered its stance, announcing that it no longer accepts *Thoughts* in its entirety because it "cannot remain eternally valid." Bhagwat declared that the only writings by Golwalkar that the RSS still considers authoritative are those it has collected and republished in the book *MS Golwalkar: His Vision and Mission*.

This pick and choose approach represents what Bal calls "a sleight of hand typical of the Sangh." While dropping the description of non-Hindus as "traitors," for instance, the book laments that some Indians have "even changed their religion" and adopted the "religion of foreigners." The "essence of our nation is spiritual," writes Golwalkar. "Without the foundation of dharma, our country has no future." Declaring that the "living principles of the Hindu society are the living systems of this nation," he proclaims: "In short, this is [a] Hindu nation." While such remarks remain enough to expose the RSS's ongoing commitment to Golwalkar's xenophobic vision, its newfound image consciousness means that the days are gone when its ideologues openly praised European fascists or overtly called non-Hindus "traitors" and members of "foreign races" who must be stripped of citizen's rights. "The dark underpinning of RSS ideology — its vision of cultural nationalism premised on the exclusion of minorities — has been smoothened for public consumption," writes Bal. Today, rather than explicitly detailing its ideology, the RSS focuses on fine-tuning its public image and controlling how it is perceived.

Consequently, Bhagwat takes the stage to announce: "We say ours is a Hindu *Rashtra*. Hindu *Rashtra* does not mean it has no place for Muslims. The day it is said that Muslims are unwanted here, the concept of Hindutva will cease to exist." Such remarks inspire commentators to discuss how the RSS is charting a new course and give RSS apologists ammunition to attack the group's critics. They ignore, of course, that Bhagwat uses the same breath to say that Muslims have a place in India and that India is a Hindu nation. He also continues to advance the core concept of Hindutva: that being Indian means being Hindu. Thus he argues: "Hinduism is not some form of worship or some language. Hinduism is the name of a cultural legacy which is of all people living in India." The word "Hindu," he says, "is an identity of the people of this region, not their religion."

Meanwhile, Golwalkar's influence still predominates over the RSS and its members. When Bhagwat speaks to mass RSS rallies, he invariably does so while standing before a huge, usually garlanded photo of Golwalkar — whose picture also hangs on the walls of the RSS headquarters in Nagpur. Modi names Golwalkar as one of his primary inspirations, calling him a "gem" and a "very great man" who is his "Guru worthy of worship." And Amit Shah has eulogized "Guruji Golwalkar" as "the one who motivated us… to serve *Maa Bharati* [Mother India]."

Shah, the driving force behind the CAA and the NRC, is unique in his willingness to throw caution to the wind and — international reputation be damned — openly employ obviously genocidal rhetoric. Thus, for instance, he has recently described undocumented Muslim immigrants in India as "infiltrators" and "termites." Shah believes it's necessary to protect against — to quote Hedgewar — the "daily onslaughts" by these "outsiders." With Shah at the helm, it's no surprise that people like Arundhati Roy are warning that the CAA/NRC combine "eerily resembles the 1935 Nuremberg Laws of the Third Reich."

What is the future of the RSS?

Its leadership reports it has been growing at "unprecedented" rates. "It must continuously keep growing," declared Hedgewar. "Our goal can be achieved only if the organization grows continuously and rapidly." It has grown so rapidly that Bhagwat, in 2018, said he can "prepare military personnel within three days, something the Army would do in 6-7 months." In fact, taking over India's military appears to be one of its next major goals. In Uttar Pradesh, it has opened its first "Army school" to "train children to become officers in the armed forces."

Whatever the future holds, one thing is obvious: under the RSS regime in India today, the fascist vision of the founding fathers of the Hindu nationalist movement is swiftly being implemented with deadly consequences and, the longer that the RSS rules the roost, the deadlier those consequences will be.

Originally published by The Polis Project [ThePolisProject.com].

— 6 —
Pulwama: A Present Moment in the Longer Kashmir Story

12 February 2019

While the bodies of the 40 Central Reserve Police Force (CRPF) troops who died in the Pulwama district of Jammu and Kashmir on Valentine's Day are only just now being laid to rest, unrest prevails throughout the Indian subcontinent in the wake of the deadliest attack on Indian security forces in the world's hottest nuclear flashpoint in 30 years.

Sabers are rattling. India has stripped Pakistan of "most favored nation" status and imposed a 200 percent tariff on all Pakistani imports. The sanctions evoke the economic adage that when goods don't cross borders, soldiers will. Various Indian television personalities are demanding war. Neither Pakistan's disavowal and denouncement of the attack nor the fact that the alleged attacker was a young Kashmiri who reportedly became a militant after being profiled, detained, and beaten in the streets by Indian police register as data points in India's present dialogues.

The only people who appear to be taking into account the Kashmiri identity of the attacker are mobs who, fielded by militant Hindu nationalist organizations like Vishwa Hindu Parishad (VHP), are attacking innocent Kashmiri Muslims throughout India.

Dehradun, a city located in the Himalayan foothills just 45 kilometers from the hippie hotspot of Rishikesh, is one notable example. Chanting "shoot the traitors," mobs of hundreds besieged Kashmiri students who took refuge in their university hostels. One female student said they appealed to the police for help but were told they should instead apologize to the mobs. Other students were seized and beaten. Although some of the assaults were caught on camera — and show officers standing by passively observing — police denied the occurrence of any incidents of violence. Students, said police, "are making a big deal out of nothing."

Meanwhile, Prime Minister Narendra Modi, who was already mobilizing to fight for BJP supremacy in the Indian General Elections later this year, urged voters in Uttar Pradesh (India's most populous state) to back his religious nationalist Bharatiya Janata Party (BJP) to guarantee a "strong government" which will give "glory on the international stage." His comments came just a day after the Pulwama attack.

The Pulwama attack set a new record, surpassing that previously set by the 2016 attack in Jammu and Kashmir's Uri district. Nineteen Indian Army soldiers died in the Uri attack. Then, just as now, Pakistan denied involvement.

Nevertheless, India insisted the attack was Pakistani orchestrated and claims it launched retaliatory "surgical strikes" against alleged militant bases inside Pakistani territory. Pakistan denies the strikes even occurred. Yet the Indian narrative was etched in celluloid in the Bollywood film "Uri: The Surgical Strike," which is still playing in India's theaters after its release last month. As a columnist for TheWire.in commented, "The film's timing will help the BJP market the surgical strike in the 2019 elections as its unique contribution to Indian security."

What is not unique about the BJP is its commitment to continuing the conflict over Kashmir, even at the risk of provoking nuclear war with Pakistan. Clutching Kashmir tighter and closer to its chest, even as its inhabitants struggle against the unwanted attention and scream that they are being stifled, has been the approach of the Indian Central Government since 1947. Escalation rather than re-evaluation is India's singular policy towards the region.

When the colonial British ignored all organic borders of language and ethnicity to partition the entire subcontinent into just two outsized territories, they set the stage for one of the most intractable and longest-lasting religio-political conflicts in modern history. Demarcating Pakistan as a Muslim State, they (perhaps inadvertently) bolstered India's burgeoning Hindu nationalist movement and its sense of self-justification in pressing for "equal treatment" by demanding a Hindu State. Since no one not belonging to the State Religion (whether official or de facto) wanted to be stranded in that state, the partition sparked the largest mass migration in history.

The two-way migration was besot by acts of horrendous violence. No one really knows how many died, but estimates range from a few hundred thousand to two million. Jammu and Kashmir, then an independent monarchy, was among the worst affected areas.

Above the Kashmir Valley, in the hills of Jammu, cadres of the Hindu nationalist paramilitary Rashtriya Swayamsevak Sangh (RSS) joined hands with the monarch, Maharaja Hari Singh, to ethnically cleanse the region of Muslims. The death toll was up to 100,000. On 26 October 1947, two weeks after the violence began and four days after India and Pakistan went to war with each other over the region, the Hindu maharaja ceded control of his still Muslim majority kingdom to the freshly-formed country of India.

The territory has remained disputed ever since, and served as fuel to the fire of nationalist fervor throughout the subcontinent as the governments of both India and Pakistan treat the land as a feather which belongs in the cap of one nation alone. Caught in the crossfire are the Kashmiri people themselves, whose lives seem subordinate to the pride of maintaining "territorial integrity." Thus, India currently keeps a minimum of half a million troops lodged in the midst of the region's 13 million residents.

In 1987, Jammu and Kashmir emerged from nearly a year of President's Rule — in which the Central Government dissolves the state legislature and imposes direct governance — to hold elections. Amidst allegations that the Indian National Congress (INC) rigged the polls to defeat candidates sympathetic to independence, anger boiled over into mass street demonstrations.

On 19 January 1990, New Delhi again imposed President's Rule. Protests increased, and on the 21st, CRPF troops cut off protesters at Gawkadal Bridge in Srinigar, the region's largest city. Opening fire, the troops gunned down at least 50 civilians — some say over 100.

Protests again increased, with hundreds of thousands and up to a million demonstrating at a time. Many abandoned protesting for militancy. Later that year, Delhi imposed the Armed Forces (Special Powers) Act, granting immunity to security forces for acts committed on duty, even atrocities.

As the militancy continued throughout the 1990s, the atrocities escalated.

Indian security forces massacred people, disappeared, tortured, raped, killed in custody, looted, destroyed houses, burned religious structures, desecrated religious books, and generally waged total war.

In 1995, Kashmiri human rights attorney Jalil Andrabi traveled to the United Nations in Geneva to appeal for intervention. Noting that "more than 40,000 people have been killed," he asserted, "These atrocities being committed on the people of Kashmir are not mere aberrations. These are part of deliberate and systematic state policy." In March 1996, Andrabi was picked up by the Indian Army while driving with his wife near his Srinigar home. Twenty days later, his body, tied up in a sack, washed ashore on the Jhelum River. His hands were tied behind his back, eyes gouged out, facial bones crushed. He had been killed with a gunshot to the head.

As the insurgency subsided in the early 2000s, a larger pattern of state-sponsored human rights abuses began coming into light.

In 2008, Amnesty International reported the discovery of mass graves, many of them concentrated in Uri district. Thousands of mass graves containing thousands of bodies have been uncovered over the years since. And mass demonstrations again grew.

Since 2010, India has resorted to "non-lethal" methods of crowd control such as pellet guns, blinding hundreds of civilians, including children. Sometimes, troops even embrace less conventional methods, as in 2017 when an Indian Army major lashed a protester to his jeep to use as a human shield. Meanwhile, on a societal level, there are efforts to inspire Muslim flight which are, in spirit, reminiscent of the RSS collaboration with Maharaja Hari Singh in 1947.

In January 2018, with the goal of driving out a local nomadic Muslim community, several men (including at least one police officer) abducted an eight-year-old girl near Kathua, a city known as the gateway to Jammu and Kashmir. They locked her in a temple owned by one of them, and gang-raped her for days before murdering her and dumping her body. When they were arrested, the BJP's State Secretary organized a protest march for their release. Joining the march were two BJP State Ministers. They had, they later said, been instructed to attend by their party leadership.

In the heat of the moment, as the BJP campaigns for re-election, mobs attack Kashmiris, and pundits call for war, beating drums and rattling sabers seems to be a far more popular approach than consideration of the history that brought South Asia to this point. Yet it's the same stale strategy. Escalation, never reevaluation.

Originally published by AntiWar.com.

— 7 —
Jammu and Kashmir Loses "Special Status": The Hindu Nationalist Agenda

8 August 2019

Terror grips the most militarized zone in the world after India's Central Government terminated Jammu and Kashmir's 70-year-old "special status" as the first step towards stripping the disputed region of statehood entirely.

Internationally infamous as the world's hottest potential nuclear flashpoint, J&K originally acceded to India in 1947 only on the condition that the newly-formed country be restricted from interfering in the domestic affairs of the mountainous northern region. The agreement was sealed between the last king of J&K, Maharaja Hari Singh Dogra, and the representative of the British crown, Governor-General Lord Mountbatten. In 1949, when passage of the constitution formed the Republic of India, the Maharaja's conditions for accession were enshrined in Article 370.

The crux of the article — in combination with Article 35A of 1954 — was that, while J&K accepted India's handling of issues like defense and foreign policy, the state otherwise reserved the right to autonomy in handling its domestic affairs. Kashmiris, thus, lived under their own distinct laws. Notably, citizens of other parts of India were prohibited from settling permanently or owning property in Kashmir. In the eyes of many Kashmiris, this prevented settler colonialism. On 5 August 2019, the President of India abolished this "special status" by decree.

Simultaneously, Home Minister Amit Shah — charged with India's internal security — introduced a bill in the upper house of parliament to strip J&K of statehood, downgrade it to a "Union Territory," and partition the region.

As Shah did this, the Central Government shut down Kashmir. It imposed a virtual curfew, banning movement of the public, shuttering educational institutions, and barring all public assemblies or meetings. It severed communications, cutting off phone and internet access. And it conducted arrests of mainstream Kashmiri political leaders — such as former chief ministers Mehbooba Mufti and Omar Abdullah — on unknown charges.

India's ruling Bharatiya Janata Party, which was just re-elected in May, campaigned on promises to scrap J&K's "special status." The BJP's manifesto alleged that it was "an obstacle in the development of the state," while Shah insisted it stood in the way of of Kashmir becoming an "integral party of India permanently" and was necessary for "national security." Indeed, the tumultuous region has suffered a significant influx in violence in recent years.

Since 2014, when Prime Minister Modi's regime first came to power, terrorist incidents in J&K have nearly tripled and security forces deaths have nearly doubled. According to a July 2019 UN report, independent bodies documented 159 security forces deaths in 2018 — a figure comparable to US troop fatalities in Iraq in 2009. The latest round of escalating tensions traces back to at least 2010, when mass protests erupted over an "encounter killing" of three civilians by Indian Army troops. Protests again erupted in 2016. During suppression efforts, security forces killed hundreds of protesters.

The Central Government has responded by flooding J&K with more and more soldiers. The small region — slightly smaller than the United Kingdom — is already occupied by a bare minimum of 500,000 troops. Since late

July 2019, India has deployed nearly another 50,000.

Delhi has additionally responded by repeatedly dissolving J&K's elected state government, imposing direct rule three times since 2015. The last time was in June 2018, after India's ruling BJP withdrew from a coalition with then J&K Chief Minister Mufti — apparently because she advocated "reconciliation" instead of a "muscular security policy" as the most effective solution to the Kashmir conflict. Elections have not been allowed since 2014.

The ongoing occupation as well as the long-term use of direct rule — imposed for approximately ten of the past 42 years — contribute to the perception of Kashmiris that they are nothing more than vassals within the Republic of India.

The religious dimensions of the conflict reinforce that perspective. With a 68 percent Muslim population, many residents of J&K have historically felt like Muslim subjects governed by Hindu rulers. Their sentiments are enhanced by the authoritative agenda so abruptly implemented by the Hindu nationalist BJP, many of whose leaders have openly demanded that India be officially declared a Hindu Nation.

To understand the present situation, it is necessary to briefly examine the longer history of the region — including how it became what MK Gandhi called "a Hindu State, the majority of its people being Muslims."

Religious conflict between ruler and ruled — as well as the sense that Kashmir is an object to be haggled over, traded, and valued only for the bragging rights of ownership — has persisted since at least the mid-19th century.

Islam took root in Kashmir in 1320 when the local king converted. By the end of the 1400s, most Kashmiris were Muslims. In 1586, the Mughal Empire sent a Hindu general, Bhagwant Das, to annex the region. He succeeded, writes 17th-century Dutch East India Company merchant Francisco Pelsaert, "by craft and subtlety, the lofty mountains and difficult roads rendering forcible conquest impossible." Mughal Emperors then adopted Kashmir as their summer resort. Meanwhile, Pelsaert records, Kashmiris remained "for the most part poor." In 1751, Afghanistan invaded and conquered Kashmir.

Kashmir's situation changed in the 1800s. As the Mughal Empire crumbled, the young Sikh community in Punjab — immediately south of J&K — asserted itself militarily. The Sikhs fought invasions of Afghanis and Persians, waged war against the Mughals, and battled local Hindu kings. Finally, they established the Sikh Empire in 1801. In 1808, the Sikh Empire annexed Jammu and then, in 1819, attacked and overthrew the Afghani occupiers of Kashmir.

The Sikh Empire was then the only major region of the Indian subcontinent which the British had not colonized. Its downfall began when the Dogra brothers gained political control. Dhian Singh Dogra was made prime minister in 1818 and Gulab Singh Dogra was made raja of Jammu in 1822. From 1840 to 1845, they staged two coups, eventually installing a child on the throne.

In 1846, when the British invaded in 1846, Gulab — then prime minister — negotiated the Sikh Empire's surrender. Shah Mohammad, a contemporary Punjabi poet, says Gulab "was serving none but himself" as he "paid obeisance" to the British "with all obsequiousness" and brought them in "by the arm." The outcome was the 1846 Treaty of Lahore. The treaty included a reward for Gulab's assistance in bringing the Sikh Empire to its knees — kingship over J&K. "After getting Kashmir in the bargain, Gulab Singh repaired forthwith to Jammu," writes

Mohammad.

Gulab was the first Maharaja of the Dogra dynasty that controlled J&K until the last Maharaja, Hari Singh Dogra, acceded the region to independent India.

The distinguishing feature of Dogra rule was exclusive state-patronage of Hinduism and a systematic campaign to Hinduize Kashmir. In her book, Hindu Rulers, Muslim Subjects, historian Mridu Rai explains that Gulab "was careful to emphasize his standing as a Hindu ruler" and publicly "denounced Hindu-Muslim marriages and conversions from Hinduism to Islam." His son, Ranbir, began "construction of a Hindu state" and founded a government department "with the single aim of securing the glorification of the Hindu religion in the state." Ranbir further "acclaimed the importance of being Hindu in order to rule in Jammu and Kashmir." His son, Pratap, represented "the interests of only the small Hindu segment of his Kashmiri subjects."

The situation had not changed by the time Pratap's nephew, Hari, came to the throne in 1925.

Global changes that year, however, saw the rise of ethnocentrism and fascism. In the US, over 30,000 members of the Ku Klux Klan marched on Washington, DC. In Italy, Mussolini made himself dictator. In Germany, Hitler published *Mein Kampf*, reformulated the Nazi Party, and founded the SS. And in India, KB Hedgewar founded the Rashtriya Swayamsevak Sangh, a uniformed paramilitary which soon drew inspiration from both Hitler and Mussolini.

In 1939, as World War II dawned with the Nazi invasion of Poland, RSS leader — soon to be chief — MS Golwalkar published a manifesto.

"We, Hindus," he writes, are "at war at once with the

Moslems." He declared that, "ever since that evil day, when Moslems first landed in [India], right up to the present moment the Hindu Nation has been gallantly fighting on to shake off the despoilers." Praising Nazi Germany for having "boldly vindicated" the "Nation Idea," he invoked the topic of "German Race Pride," writing, "To keep up the purity of the race and its culture, Germany shocked the world by her purging the country of the Semitic races — the Jews. Race pride at its highest has been manifested here. Germany has also shown how well-nigh impossible it is for races and cultures, having differences going to the root, to be assimilated into one united whole, a good lesson for us in Hindustan to learn and profit by."

Meanwhile, Kashmiri Muslims languished in the Hindu state constructed by the Dogras.

In 1941, nearly 80 percent of the population of the princely state of J&K was Muslim. Yet, writes political scientist Sumantra Bose, "Local Muslims were barred from becoming officers in the princely state's military forces and were almost nonexistent in the civil administration." Bose quotes a Kashmiri Hindu activist of the time, who said, "The poverty of the Muslim masses is appalling. Dressed in rags and barefoot, a Muslim peasant presents the appearance of a starving beggar.... Most are landless laborers, working as serfs for absentee landlords."

With the conclusion of WWII, and the success of the independence movement, the Indian subcontinent finally secured its freedom from the yoke of the British Empire in 1947.

By then, the RSS had penetrated every major area of the subcontinent and boasted up to a half a million members. In J&K, Maharaja Hari Singh Dogra was left with a decision — join his state to Muslim-majority

Pakistan, to Hindu-majority India, or remain independent. As he weighed his options, Golwalkar visited the Maharaja on 17 October 1947 to pressure him to join India.

In the days and weeks before Golwalkar's visit, the Dogra's troops and the RSS joined hands to conduct a state-sanctioned pogrom of Muslims.

In the mountains of Jammu, Muslims constituted a smaller majority than in the Kashmir Valley to the north. In September, they were targeted for ethnic cleansing. "The Dogra state troops were at the forefront of attacks on Muslims," writes historian Ilyas Chattha. "The state authorities were also reported to be issuing arms... to local volunteer organizations such as RSS." Chattha claims, "The Maharaja of the Dogra Hindu state was complicit in the targeted violence against Kashmiri Muslims." According to some reports, he explains, Hari Singh Dogra was 'in person commanding all the forces' which were ethnically cleansing the Muslims."

"Instead of trying to prevent such killings and preserving communal peace, the Maharaja's administration helped and even armed the communal marauders," writes Ved Bhasin, a witness to the massacre who later became a journalist. "It was a planned genocide by the RSS activists."

After the Maharaja agreed to accession on 26 October — barely a week after RSS chief Golwalkar's visit — the killings continued. "In the first week of November, the Pakistan government dispatched many buses to Jammu city to transport the refugees into Sialkot," writes Chattha. The Dogra's troops and RSS men "attacked the caravan and killed most of the passengers and abducted their women."

By the end, the total number of dead was catastrophically high. Bhasin says, "There is no doubt that their number runs into several thousands." Political scientist Christopher Snedden says, "Perhaps between 20,000 and 100,000 Muslims were killed." A 1948 report in London's *The Times* alleged that "237,000 Muslims were systematically exterminated."

However many actually died, one tragic fact stood out. "There was hardly any family in the region which escaped the horrible wrath of communal hooligans," writes journalist Zafar Choudhary. "The events of 1947 permanently changed the way the Muslims of Jammu would live or think. A majority of them was either massacred, or pushed to the other side of the divide; many fled to save their lives thus leaving behind a terrorized and harassed minuscule minority."

In 1949, British civil servant William Barton, writing in *Foreign Affairs* magazine, warned that a "militant group" called the RSS, "whose object is to absorb Pakistan, has of late been asserting itself." He noted the "atrocities committed" during the "wholesale expulsion of Moslems from the Jammu province." Barton added, "One wonders whether the Indian Government has considered the military implications of the retention of Kashmir in India. With half or more of the population hostile… it would have to maintain an army of occupation."

India had already begun dealing with the ramifications of retaining Kashmir. On 22 October 1947, four days before the accession, India and Pakistan commenced their first of three wars over the region. Ever since, the two South Asian nations have incessantly squabbled over J&K as though it were a crown jewel.

In 1965, the second war over Kashmir claimed the lives of perhaps 7,000 troops — no one seems to have kept count of how many civilians died. The war ended in a stalemate.

Yet the RSS's Golwalkar was ecstatic.

In his 1966 manifesto, Golwalkar proclaimed, "The nation's pulse has been quickened by an unprecedented upsurge of patriotic pride and self-respect. Verily this is the first and the foremost lesson that the war has taught us." Analogizing the conflict to a mythological battle between the Hindu god Ram and a demon, he argued, "It is inevitable to annihilate the support — the evil persons — if we have to do away with evil." This, he implied, required absorbing Pakistan into India. Demanding "the hoisting of our flag in Lahore and other parts of Pakistan," he declared, "Since times immemorial, those areas have formed integral parts of our motherland.... Our fight for independence can be deemed to have come to a successful close only when we liberate all those areas now under enemy occupation."

"Jammu and Kashmir has been a focal point for Hindu nationalism ever since Partition," writes political scientist Christophe Jaffrelot. "For the ideologues of this movement, as for so many Indians, the state became the bone of contention par excellence with Pakistan.... For the Hindu nationalists the state was inseparably a part of India." In the 1950s, this contention produced calls for *Akhand Bharat* — an undivided Indian subcontinent whose hypothetical borders variously include Afghanistan, Bangladesh, Myanmar, Pakistan, Sri Lanka and Tibet.

The demand to "restore the natural extension of the sacred land that is Bharat," as Jaffrelot phrases it, gained a political infrastructure in 1951 with the founding of the Bharatiya Jana Sangh — the precursor to the BJP and the RSS's first political wing.

In 1952, the BJS's founder and president announced his commitment to full annexation of J&K. "Part of India is today in the occupation of the enemy," declared Syama

Prasad Mukherjee. "Is there any possibility of our getting back this territory? We shall not get it through the efforts of the United Nations: we shall not get it through peaceful methods, by negotiations with Pakistan. That means we lose it, unless we use force.... I am a communalist, I am a reactionary, I am a war-monger." In 1953, Mukherjee made the issue a hill to die on — literally — when he launched an agitation in concert with the RSS-founded Jammu Praja Parishad, illegally entered Kashmir, was arrested, and died in jail of a heart attack.

The BJS never had much electoral success, but it remained devoted to Mukherjee's vision. Over the years, its presidents included Prem Nath Dogra and Balraj Madhok — founding fathers of J&K's RSS branch. And in 1965, in the midst of war, the BJS passed a resolution proclaiming, "*Akhand Bharat* will be a reality, unifying India and Pakistan."

In 1980, the BJS was reformulated as the BJP with its last two presidents — lifetime RSS workers AB Vajpayee and LK Advani — at the helm.

The BJP's 1984 manifesto called for "deleting" Article 370, a demand Advani advanced at the party's 1986 convention. Its 1996 manifesto aggressively supported "reclaiming the portion of our territory which has been illegally held by Pakistan," describing J&K as a "strategic border state" that has "emerged as the principal challenge to Indian nationhood." That year, Advani's protégé, the late Sushma Swaraj, reiterated demands for "the abolishment of Article 370" in a speech in parliament. The issue was largely shelved in 1998 — the year the BJP first gained national power — but it has been pressed by every party manifesto since 2009.

Former RSS spokesperson turned BJP mouthpiece Ram

Madhav recently wrote that abolishing Article 370 "has been a running theme of the BJP and Jana Sangh." Its existence, he insisted, led to "lack of development, progress, and prosperity." Yet earlier remarks by Madhav suggest the real motive behind the BJP's lightning-swift action on J&K may be commitment to Golwalkar's call for "hoisting of our flag" in Pakistan. In 2015, speaking in Oxford, he declared, "The RSS still believes that one day these parts, which have for historical reasons separated only 60 [sic] years ago, will again, through popular goodwill, come together and *Akhand Bharat* will be created. The RSS believes in that, and as an RSS member, I also hold on to that view."

That view is already being openly propagated in India's parliament.

"Today, we have reclaimed Jammu and Kashmir," said MP Sanjay Raut, a member of Shiv Sena, a regional Hindu nationalist party allied with the BJP. Speaking in the upper-house of parliament on 5 August, he concluded, "Tomorrow, we will take Baluchistan, Pakistan-occupied Kashmir, and I have trust that this government will fulfill the dream of undivided India."

Pursuing that dream may produce a nightmare.

On 6 August, India's lower-house of parliament ratified Amit Shah's "Jammu and Kashmir Reorganisation Bill, 2019," stripping J&K of statehood and partitioning it.

The same day, Pakistani Prime Minister Imran Khan addressed a joint session of parliament in his country. "With an approach of this nature, incidents like Pulwama are bound to happen again," Khan warned, referring to the February 2019 suicide attack in Kashmir that left 40 Indian security forces dead. He added, "This will be a war that no one will win and the implications will be global."

Meanwhile, what do Kashmiris want for Kashmir? No one knows. They are entirely cut off from the rest of the world. Forget about the freedom to express their hopes and desires for the future of Kashmir. They are banned from even accessing basic communications. They cannot speak to the media, they cannot speak to anyone inside or outside of India, and they cannot speak to any of their friends and family members living outside Kashmir.

As the BJP — cheered on by the RSS — expedites its J&K strategy, Kashmiris are denied the right to offer their opinion on the Kashmir solution.

That is as per the vision of the RSS's Golwalkar. "To say that Kashmiris shall determine their own future is to repudiate the oneness of the country," he writes. Thus, just as for the past several centuries, Kashmiris remain restricted from controlling their own political destinies.

Originally published by AntiWar.com.

— 8 —
Socializing With The RSS: German Diplomat's "Direct Contact" Approach?

22 July 2019

Germany's Ambassador to India, Sir Walter J Lindner, shocked countless Indians by meeting with Rashtriya Swayamsevak Sangh (RSS) chief Mohan Bhagwat on 17 July 2019 at the RSS headquarters in Nagpur, Maharashtra — posing beneath a portrait of MS Golwalkar.

Seventy years earlier, Golwalkar was just about to become chief of the RSS. "To keep up the purity of the race and its culture, Germany shocked the world by her purging the country of the Semitic races — the Jews," he wrote in his 1939 manifesto, *We, or Our Nationhood Defined*. He penned those words at the dawn of the Second World War which began as Nazi Germany launched its invasion of Poland.

Lindner, 62, was appointed as ambassador just three months ago. Described as "unorthodox," he first visited India in 1977 as a backpacker. He is learning Hindi, calls himself an artist, wears a pony-tail (an unusual choice in a suit-and-tie oriented Western world), and believes that diplomats should reflect on "broad society." He expresses commitment to transparency, commenting, "In some countries where the press is not free, social media is the only way of communicating. I think it's also a great way for today's diplomacy. Earlier, diplomacy was all about something done by grey eminences behind closed doors.... Today's diplomacy has to be different: closer to the people and more approachable for the young generation."

True to form, Lindner transparently shared pictures of

his visit with Bhagwat on Twitter. Calling the RSS "the world's largest voluntary organization," he added that it was "not uncontroversially perceived throughout its history." That is putting it diplomatically.

By his own admission, though, Lindner doesn't use that sort of rhetoric. "Normally a diplomat would talk diplomatic language," he says. "Forget this. You won't hear diplomatic language from me. We will go right to the heart of the matter." Going right to the heart of the matter, therefore, let's consider why — ideologically — the RSS is "not uncontroversially perceived."

After its inception in 1925, RSS leaders like Golwalkar repeatedly expressed admiration for Nazi racial policies, continuing to do so throughout Adolf Hitler's rise to power. The mentor of RSS founder KB Hedgewar — BS Moonje — was also enamored by Europe's fascist movements. Upon traveling to meet Italian dictator Benito Mussolini in Rome in 1931, Moonje analogized the RSS to Mussolini's fascist outfits.

Specifically praising the Opera Nazionale Balilla (a fascist youth group) for its contribution to "the military regeneration of Italy," Moonje wrote, "India and particularly Hindu India need some such institution for the military regeneration of the Hindus." Rhapsodizing about how "the idea of fascism vividly brings out the conception of unity amongst people," he declared: "Our institution of Rashtriya Swayamsevak Sangh of Nagpur under Dr Hedgewar is of this kind."

When Hedgewar died in 1940, the leadership of the RSS passed to Golwalkar. Like his predecessor's mentor, he too was fascinated by Mussolini's Italy — as well as Nazi Germany — and compared the RSS's goals to those of both fascist countries.

"Look at Italy," wrote Golwalkar. "The old Roman Race consciousness of conquering the whole territory round the Mediterranean Sea, so long dormant, has roused itself, and shaped the Racial-National aspirations accordingly. The ancient Race spirit, which prompted the Germanic tribes to over-run the whole of Europe, has re-risen in modern Germany with the result that the Nation perforce follows aspirations, predetermined by the traditions left by its depredatory ancestors."

European fascists, he believed, demonstrated the right to define nationality by race.

Thus, he continued, "Even so with us: our Race spirit has once again roused itself." As a result, he insisted that there belonged to "every Race the indisputable right of excommunicating from its Nationality all those who, having been of the Nation, for ends of their own, turned traitors and entertained aspirations contravening or differing from those of the National Race as a whole."

The "National Race," in Golwalkar's mind, was the "Hindu Race." The only "nationalist patriots," he wrote, are those "with the aspiration to glorify the Hindu race and Nation next to their heart." And who were "traitors" to the nation?

In his 1966 book, *Bunch of Thoughts*, he explained that anyone who converted away from Hinduism was a "traitor," writing, "So we see that it is not merely a case of change of faith, but a change even in national identity. What else is it, if not treason, to join the camp of the enemy leaving their mother-nation in the lurch?"

Lindner, of course, may not have read Golwalkar or Moonje.

Yet as a diplomat qualified to represent Germany in India, he is undoubtedly aware of the dialogues concerning the origins of the RSS — even, of course, noting that it is "not uncontroversially perceived."

Like any outside visitor to India (especially one from Germany), he has probably also noticed the tall stacks of Hitler's manifesto, *Mein Kampf*, which are piled high at the entrances of many mall bookstores. Media periodically reports how that book sells in the hundreds of thousands in India; as of this writing, it sits at #72 of the top 100 best-selling book on Amazon India.

As Germany, nearly 75 years after the end of World War II, still struggles to fully exorcise the specter of Nazi Germany — even banning the use of the Nazi swastika and other associated symbols as well as prosecuting former death camp guards like Johann Rehbogen, 95, as recently as last year — the German ambassador ought to reckon with Golwalkar's praise for Nazi racial policy.

"Race pride at its highest has been manifested here," wrote Golwalkar in reference to the Nazi purge of the Jews. "Germany has also shown how well-nigh impossible it is for races and cultures, having differences going to the root, to be assimilated into one united whole, a good lesson for us in Hindustan to learn and profit by."

Beyond endorsing the purge, Golwalkar mirrored Hitler's rhetoric about racial superiority, "national consciousness," character-building, self-restraint, sacrifice for the fatherland, and the reunification of defunct territorial entities.

"From childhood," wrote Hitler in *Mein Kampf* in 1925, the "entire education and development" of a "young fellow citizen" should be "directed at giving him the conviction of being absolutely superior to the others." Golwalkar, in *Bunch of Thoughts*, declared that "the average man of this country was at one time incomparably superior to the average man of the other lands."

Hitler lamented that, in the past, "Germany did not possess enough national consciousness and also ruthlessness."

Golwalkar in *We, or Our Nationhood Defined*, proclaimed, "National consciousness blazes forth and we Hindus rally to the Hindu Standard, the *Bhagwa Dhwaja*, set our teeth in grim determination to wipe out the opposing forces."

"With his physical force and skill," argued Hitler, the German "has again to win the belief in the invincibility of his entire nationality." To achieve "national prosperity," Golwalkar argued, "the first thing is invincible physical strength."

Hitler wrote, "The folkish State, in its work of education, has, besides the physical training, to put the greatest emphasis on the training of the character."

Golwalkar wrote, "Physical strength is necessary, but character is more important."

Hitler claimed, "If in our public schools one had instilled into our young people a little less knowledge and a little more self-restraint, this would have been amply rewarded." Golwalkar claimed, "The discipline nurtured in the Sangh is the spontaneous self-restraint of a cultured people."

Hitler praised the "thousands upon thousands of young Germans" who "bring their young lives as sacrifices to the altar of the beloved fatherland."

Golwalkar declared, "To offer one's all, even his dearest possessions, at the altar of motherland is the first and foremost duty of every son of this soil." Hitler urged, "We must struggle for the existence of our fatherland, our national unity."

Golwalkar lamented, "Consciousness of the unity of our motherland has all but disappeared from our mind."

Furthermore, Hitler — who wanted to reestablish Germany's past broad territorial sway — proclaimed, "What must guide us constantly today is the fundamental insight that the regaining of lost imperial territories is primarily a question of regaining the political independence and power of the motherland."

He called for "the reuniting of the unhappy oppressed portions with the motherland."

Golwalkar, for his part, deplored the loss of "integral parts of our motherland." He claimed, "Reunification of those parts with Bharat would therefore be a welcome development and an act of liberation for them."

Golwalkar understood Hitler's goal of territorial expansion, writing, "Germany strove, and has to a great extent achieved what she strove for, to once again bring under one sway the whole of the territory, hereditarily possessed by the Germans but which, as a result of political disputes, had been portioned off as different countries under different states."

Today, the RSS routinely enflames tensions by echoing Golwalkar's thoughts about "hereditary" territory. As recently as March 2019, for instance, RSS executive Indresh Kumar commented, "People used to say there was no Pakistan before 1947. Till 1045 AD, the area was called Hindustan. It will become Hindustan again after 2025."

In May 2019, immediately after he was appointed ambassador, Lindner had said that Germany is willing to back India in its fight against terrorism. That worthy goal, however, may be hampered in efficacy and appear inconsistent in approach, considering his visit with Bhagwat.

After all, one of the primary goals of any diplomat is to work for peace. Yet the RSS, whose founders left a legacy of divisive ideology and whose modern guides are often accused of instigating communal conflict, has also faced accusations of 'tolerating terrorist attacks'.

Swami Aseemanand, an RSS *pracharak* (full-time worker), is one of the most egregious examples. Between 2006 and 2008, he was implicated in multiple bombings of Muslim targets — most notably the Samjhauta Express, the "peace train" connecting Delhi to Lahore. In 2010, he was arrested in connection with the terrorist incidents; in 2012, he confessed his involvement in interviews with *Caravan* magazine.

Aseemanand, in those interviews, claims that he discussed his plans at a meeting with Mohan Bhagwat, Indresh Kumar, and others.

"It's very important that it be done," he alleges Bhagwat and Kumar told him. "But don't link it to the Sangh. The Sangh will not do this…. If you will do this, we will be at ease with this…. If you do it, then people won't say that we committed a crime for the sake of committing a crime. It will be connected to the ideology."

Meanwhile, neo-Nazism is making a resurgence in Germany alongside the rise of the Alternative for Germany (AfD) political party. In June 2019, Thomas Haldenwang, head of the country's domestic security agency, stated, "We currently have 12,700 rightwing extremists willing to use violence in Germany." One of those is Stephan Ernst, who assassinate Christian Democratic Union (CDU) municipal politician Walter Lübcke on 2 June.

Subsequently, the CDU announced its refusal to ever consider alliance with AfD when forming a government. "Anyone who makes a case for a rapprochement or even cooperation with the AfD must know that he is seeking rapprochement with a party that consciously tolerates far-right thinking, anti-Semitism and racism in its ranks," reported a CDU position paper in late June.

Elsewhere in the world, white supremacist terrorists have targeted innocent civilians with shocking lethality.

In New Zealand, for instance, Brenton Tarrant gunned down 51 Muslims in March 2019. His manifesto credits Norwegian mass shooter Anders Breivik as his "true inspiration." Breivik murdered 77 white Norwegians in July 2011 — mostly children attending a youth camp for the Norwegian Labour Party.

Breivik also left behind a manifesto. Referring to the RSS as the Sangh Parivar, he called it a "positive thing" that they "dominate the streets... and often riot and attack Muslims." However, instead of engaging in such "counter-productive" behavior, he urged them to "consolidate military cells." Terming the Sangh as a "resistance movement," he concluded: "It is essential that the European and Indian resistance movements learn from each other and cooperate as much as possible. Our goals are more or less identical."

Why, even as Germany's ruling CDU disavows the legitimacy of German right-wing political parties like the AfD, would the country's ambassador to India countenance an ideological outfit like the RSS — a group whose leader, Bhagwat, boasted in 2018 is capable of raising an army faster than the Indian Army.

In his unorthodox approach to diplomacy, Lindner frequently mixes and mingles with the common people of India.

"When you are a diplomat, you spend most of your time in diplomatic circles," says Lindner. "I am always trying to have direct contact with people, be it in factories or slums." He frequently shares his experiences on social media. It is a refreshing take on an all too often elitist duty.

Perhaps his meeting with the RSS was intended as such a form of "direct contact with people."

Perhaps it was not formally sanctioned by the German government, but merely an autonomous decision of his own. Diplomats are often entrusted with the power to set their own agendas — to a degree. Yet, why would he choose to fraternize with an organization with such a 'tainted' pedigree? Was he recognizing where the true power lies?

Responding to escalating criticism of his visit, Lindner insisted that he "went to educate myself about the organization," even though he is aware of "accusations of fascism" and that, as a German, "the images (of the RSS) always remind us of something." He says he asked "many questions on radicalism."

Does his defense, though, bear up to scrutiny considering that his supposedly educational trip included stopping to touch the feet of a statue of Hedgewar?

The wounds of Nazism are still healing as Germany makes ongoing reparations — on 20 July, for instance, promising up to USD 420 million in compensation to 8,000 Romanian Jewish Holocaust survivors.

Whatever his rationale, Ambassador Walter Lindner ought to consider how his visit appears in the eyes of many Indians, particularly minorities, who feel persecuted by the RSS, as well as what message it sends about modern Germany's feelings for the six million Jews slaughtered in the Holocaust.

Originally published by The Quint [TheQuint.com].

— 9 —
Ayodhya: A Symbol of Rule of Lawlessness

13 November 2019

"If you want a picture of the future, imagine a boot stamping on a human face — forever," wrote George Orwell.

Nineteen Eighty-Four is not only the title of Orwell's dystopian novel, but also the year that the future changed forever for the Republic of India. The events of that year reverberated around the world once again on 9 November 2019 when the Supreme Court of India issued a judgment in a land dispute.

For decades, India's courts kicked around various lawsuits filed by plaintiffs asserting their right of ownership to a disputed property in Ayodhya, Uttar Pradesh. The Supreme Court's final ruling came thirty years after the Hindu nationalist Vishwa Hindu Parishad (VHP) — categorized by the US Central Intelligence Agency as a "religious militant organization" — laid at the site a foundation-stone for a temple to the Hindu deity, Ram. The land belonged, the court ruled, to the infant god Ram.

Since the infant did not appear in court to take possession of his property, control passed into the hands of the Ram Janmabhoomi Nyas, a VHP-controlled trust. Yet rather than entrusting the Nyas with building a Ram Mandir (temple), the court ordered the Central Government to create a new trust to ensure construction. Thus, India's ruling Bharatiya Janata Party (BJP) apparently entered the temple-building business.

Because what began in 1984 is of monumental consequence to the present, we must peer back into the past.

In October 1984, as the ruling party in New Delhi organized a massacre of Sikhs that shook the nation to the core, the communal fuse lit by the VHP was already burning.

In April 1984, the Hindu nationalist group launched a campaign which would eventually fundamentally alter the political landscape of India. The VHP set out to gain control of the alleged birthplace of Ram, which they claimed was located in Ayodhya. They wanted to build a Ram Mandir, but faced one key challenge.

The Babri Masjid — a mosque — had stood on that location for nearly 500 years.

Before they could build, the VHP had first to destroy. So they started laying the groundwork. In October 1984, they founded a youth wing called Bajrang Dal (also now categorized by the CIA as a "religious militant organization") and began drumming up public awareness and support for the campaign by organizing *rath yatras* (chariot processions) to *Ram janmabhoomi* (Ram's birthplace) in Ayodhya.

Meanwhile, Ram Lalla — the infant deity — filed a lawsuit demanding the title to the land where the mosque stood. In July 1989, an Uttar Pradesh High Court recognized Ram Lalla as a legal entity and approved a former judge turned VHP executive to represent the deity. The god himself was, in the eyes of the courts, laying claim to the site.

By October 1989, the movement had generated riots in Meerut, Uttar Pradesh, and Bhagalpur, Bihar, that claimed the lives of well over a thousand people, mostly Muslims.

Then, on 9 November 1989, the VHP escalated the issue by laying a foundation-stone for the proposed temple on a plot of land just opposite the mosque. "To the fundamentalists, the communal bloodbath of the last few months matters little," wrote journalist Pankaj Pachauri a few weeks later. "Ashok Singhal, general secretary of the Vishwa Hindu Parishad (VHP), makes it clear that no amount of blood-letting will stop his cadres from constructing the Ram temple at the controversial site which includes a 16th century mosque."

The religious demand had already become a political one.

The BJP was formed in 1980 by *pracharaks* (full-time workers) of the Rashtriya Swayamsevak Sangh (RSS) paramilitary as a political arm to advance the RSS's Hindu supremacist agenda. In June 1989, the BJP formally joined the VHP's campaign. Religion and politics are always a volatile and inevitably explosive mix — this time was no different.

BJP President L.K. Advani led the charge in 1990.

Setting out from Gujarat on a *Ram rath yatra*, Advani rode in a minibus mocked up as Ram's chariot. Heading for Ayodhya, he plotted a circuitous 10,000 kilometer route across the heartland of the Indian subcontinent. Flanked at times by Atal Bihari Vajpayee, a member of parliament, and Narendra Modi, a RSS *pracharak*, he was trailed by thousands of *kar sevaks* (activists) from the RSS, VHP, Bajrang Dal, and other groups.

As reported by News18, "Modi was the architect of Advani's yatra plans."

The procession halted in multiple cities per day so Advani could deliver rousing speeches. His remarks were apparently over-stimulating — his swelling body of itinerant followers killed scores of Muslims along the way. The day before he was scheduled to enter Uttar Pradesh,

Advani was arrested. With the icon of the movement behind bars, anti-Muslim riots erupted in several states, leaving hundreds dead.

In Ayodhya, VHP activists surrounded and surged towards the Babri Masjid, attempting to demolish it as they erected a saffron flag atop its dome. Police intervention left approximately 20 people dead. "This episode reinforced the champion-of-Hinduism image that the BJP had been trying to acquire," wrote political scientist Christophe Jaffrelot.

It also set the stage for the drama to be fully played out.

In 1991, the BJP campaigned on a pledge to build a Ram Mandir in Ayodhya, calling it "a symbol of the vindication of our cultural heritage and national self-respect." They fell short nationally but rose to power in Uttar Pradesh. With the state government in the BJP's hands, the Babri Masjid soon came tumbling down.

On 6 December 1992, hundreds of thousands rallied around the mosque to listen to speeches by the then BJP President Murli Manohar Joshi, MP Uma Bharti and Advani. Sparked by their fiery rhetoric, an activist or two burst past police, climbed up the mosque, and once again planted a saffron flag atop it. A firestorm ensued.

"We saw them break through the first police barrier," said journalist Mark Tully, who was an eyewitness. "The police did not seem to resist them at all... I saw this sight of a police officer pushing his way through his men so that he could run away faster than the men. And the police just deserted."

Given free rein, activists swarmed the mosque. Armed with crowbars, pickaxes, sledgehammers and their bare hands, they tore apart the structure in a matter of hours — subsequently erecting a makeshift temple in its place and installing a statue of Ram Lalla.

Then came the pogroms.

Witnesses told Human Rights Watch (HRW) that the police in Ayodhya were either absent or participating when mobs of hundreds roamed the streets in the pre-dawn hours of 7 December, beating — sometimes lynching — Muslims and burning their homes and businesses. "This was not just some mindless and wanton destruction of human life and property by the *kar sevaks* in order to sustain the high they had achieved only a few hours ago by razing the Babri Masjid to the ground," one eyewitness stated. "On the contrary, they worked to a carefully crafted plan."

The flames of violence fanned across the land and were still burning bright when the new year dawned.

"The violence of the 1992-93 riots following the demolition of the Babri Masjid in Ayodhya on 6 December 1992 exceeded anything India had yet experienced since Partition," wrote Jaffrelot. Thousands — perhaps up to 3,000 — died. Most were Muslims.

In the wake of the violence, the RSS, VHP and Bajrang Dal — collectively known as the Sangh Parivar (family of organizations) — were all briefly banned, but their willingness to embrace brutality as the means to the end they desired had already set the tone for the anthem the Hindu nationalist movement continues to sing.

For Muslims, the destruction represented what international relations expert Dibyesh Anand called a "poetics of fear" where "minority Muslims have no option but to accept their subjugation or face further violence from the awakened Hindu nation." For Hindu extremists, however, it was what sociologist Prema Kurien defined as "a watershed event in the history of the Hindu nationalist movement" which "propelled the BJP and its Sangh Parivar affiliates into the limelight." As HRW reported: "The campaign to build a Ram temple at the site of the Babri Masjid in Ayodhya — which was hugely successful in cultivating a national Hindu vote bank — helped catapult the BJP into power in the early 1990s."

During the 1998 national elections, the BJP declared its commitment to facilitating construction of a "magnificent" Ram Mandir in Ayodhya. The party emerged victorious with Vajpayee as Prime Minister. Advani was tapped not only as deputy prime minister but also as Home Minister (tasked with law and order) while MM Joshi was made minister of Human Resource Development (tasked with education).

All three were RSS men.

Vajpayee was 15 years old when he joined the RSS in 1939, a year before M.S. Golwalkar took over as the second and longest-serving leader of the paramilitary.

It was the same year that Golwalkar published his infamous manifesto, *We or Our Nationhood Defined*, in which he proclaimed: "Ever since that evil day, when Moslems first landed in Hindustan, right up to the present moment, the Hindu Nation has been gallantly fighting on to shake off the despoilers." He declared that "we, Hindus, are at war at once with the Moslems" who "take themselves to be the conquering invaders and grasp for power." The "cause of our ills," he insisted, was the day that "the Moslems first tread upon this land." Yet Golwalkar saw a glimmer of hope, claiming that the Hindu "is rousing himself up again and the world has to see the might of the regenerated Hindu Nation strike down the enemy's hosts with its mighty arm."

In 1947, as India was about to become independent from the British Empire, Golwalkar visited the maharajah of the Princely State of Jammu and Kashmir to pressure him to expand his militia. His visit came within weeks of a pogrom against Muslims in Jammu in which the maharajah and the RSS collaborated to wipe out tens of thousands — or more. That was the year that Vajpayee became an RSS *pracharak*.

Despite growing up immersed in the Islamophobia of the RSS, Vajpayee's administration was generally moderate.

The BJP, unable to win an absolute majority in the 1998 elections, was forced to form a coalition with other parties. Consequently, Jaffrelot explains that it "reverted to its moderate line, discarding the manipulation of religious symbols for political purposes in favor of touting more legitimate issues such as national unity and economic independence." The party "put on the backburner contentious issues" such as the pledge to construct Ram Mandir — as well as its promise to abolish Article 370 of the Indian Constitution, which provided special status to Jammu and Kashmir.

Everything changed with the advent of Modi.

After assisting Advani's *Ram rath yatra*, Modi swiftly advanced up the BJP hierarchy. In 1998, he was rewarded with a national position as organizing secretary of the BJP. By October 2001, political wrangling in Gujarat ended in his appointment as the state's Chief Minister.

Almost immediately, the Ayodhya conflict engulfed Gujarat. Ten years after the Babri Masjid was destroyed, Modi earned the ignominious appellation of Butcher of Gujarat.

On 27 February 2002, a train filled with VHP activists was returning from Ayodhya to Gujarat when someone pulled the emergency cord. The train stopped, it was allegedly set upon by a mob of Muslims, and several coaches caught fire. Fifty-nine Hindus, mostly women and children, died in the blaze.

Modi responded by immediately (and without evidence) declaring it an act of terrorism perpetrated by the Islamic Republic of Pakistan. In a televised event, the dead were removed from the train as Modi ordered their charred corpses to be transported, uncovered, for 100 kilometers from Godhra to Ahmedabad. The dead were handed over to the VHP, which then paraded the bodies through the streets.

On 28 February, the Sangh Parivar initiated a statewide pogrom against Muslims.

As reported by HRW, the attacks "were planned, well in advance of the Godhra incident, and organized with extensive police participation." Over three days, the Sangh slaughtered thousands. "The groups most directly responsible for violence against Muslims in Gujarat include the Vishwa Hindu Parishad, the Bajrang Dal, the ruling BJP, and the umbrella organization Rashtriya Swayamsevak Sangh," reported HRW. Leaflets distributed by the VHP vowed to kill Muslims in the same way as the Babri Masjid was destroyed.

Overseeing it all was Modi, a fact repeatedly revealed by whistleblowers like BJP State Minister Haren Pandya and Deputy Commissioner of Intelligence Sanjiv Bhatt as well as participants in the pogrom who were caught fingering the chief minister on camera in a 2007 sting conducted by an Indian magazine.

VHP chief Ashok Singhal, the architect of the *Ram Janmabhoomi* movement, reportedly described the Gujarat pogrom as a "successful experiment which will be repeated all over the country." He lauded entire villages "emptied of Islam" as a "victory for Hindu society." Then, in 2003, Singhal denounced Prime Minister Vajpayee for supposedly being "the only person in the BJP and Sangh Parivar opposed to the Ram temple movement."

"The destruction of the Babri Mosque in Ayodhya on December 6, 1992, and the anti-Muslim riots in Gujarat in 2002 are two spectacular events that have been etched into the memory of Hindu nationalists as symbols of the awakened Hindu nation," wrote Anand. "These are held out as the prime illustrations of the Hindu nationalist awakening." The election of Modi was the culmination of that awakening.

The BJP was voted out of power in 2004, but returned with a roar in 2014 after Modi campaigned on his identity as a *Hindutvavadi* — an adherent of Hindutva, the religious nationalist political ideology of Hindu supremacy which guides the Sangh.

Modi's first term as prime minister was marked by a sharp rise in anti-minority violence but little in terms of advancing the Sangh's political goals on a national level. Rather, he focused on consolidating his power and stacking his cabinet with RSS men. Within six months of his reelection in May 2019, however, his government achieved the top two most controversial items on the BJP's religious nationalist agenda.

In August, the Modi regime scrapped Article 370 and stripped Jammu and Kashmir — the only Muslim majority state in India — of statehood. Boosting its troop presence by tens of thousands, instituting a communications blackout and mass-arresting the entire civil society, the BJP accomplished a full annexation of the previously mostly autonomous region.

Then, three months later, came the Ayodhya verdict.

Welcoming the verdict, RSS chief Mohan Bhagwat declared: "The building of Ram Mandir will end a major issue of friction between Hindus and Muslims." Top VHP executive Alok Kumar called it "one of the greatest judicial verdicts in the world." Yet, implying continued friction, Kumar insisted that the "judgement is not the end of the story, it is the beginning."

Friction remains over the impunity enjoyed by the Sangh after the devastation it wrought in Ayodhya. Advani, Joshi, Bharti, and several others (including Mahant Nrityagopal Das, head of the Ram Janmabhoomi Nyas) are still facing criminal conspiracy charges for the role they played in instigating — perhaps even organizing — the destruction of the Babri Masjid and the pogroms that followed it. Yet no sentence was ever passed on anyone involved in the bloodshed of 1992-1993.

The Supreme Court's verdict acknowledged that "the destruction of the mosque and the obliteration of the Islamic structure was an egregious violation of the rule of law."

In 2003, however, journalist Saba Naqvi wrote: "No court can possibly give a verdict that hands over the disputed land to the very people who wantonly destroyed the Babri Masjid." Yet the Supreme Court's Ayodhya verdict did just that. The verdict set a precedent for legitimizing a Mafia-style approach. If someone has built a house on land you want, first destroy their house. Then stage a massacre. Then ask the courts for a stamp of approval on the land-ownership demand.

The verdict represents that vision of the future in which a boot is forever stamping on a human face. "Always there will be the intoxication of power, constantly increasing and constantly growing subtler," wrote Orwell. "Always, at every moment, there will be the thrill of victory, the sensation of trampling on an enemy who is helpless." The verdict sanctions those boot-wearers who exult in crushing the downtrodden. It codifies injustice.

Ayodhya is a symbol of rule of lawlessness.

Originally published by The Polis Project [ThePolisProject.com].

— 10 —
US Election: Why Tulsi Gabbard's "Hindutva" Link Deserves Scrutiny

22 November 2019

After Tulsi Gabbard, the first Hindu to run for US president, failed to qualify for the September 2019 Democratic presidential debates, many wrote her campaign off as a lost cause.

Gabbard stuck it out. She pledged to soldier on until the Democratic Party's National Convention in July 2020. And she started making headlines — including about her alleged support from both Putin's Russia and India's Hindu nationalist movement.

The news isn't always positive but, as the saying goes, any press is good press.

"Hillary Clinton suggests Russians are 'grooming' Tulsi Gabbard for third-party run," reported CNN in mid-October. Yet Gabbard shot back, calling Clinton "the queen of warmongers" and "embodiment of corruption." By mid-November, CNN was reporting that Gabbard actually received a boost after Clinton's attacks raised her profile nationally.

Gabbard is on the rise. While she is back in the debates, her poll numbers in early voting states like New Hampshire are steadily increasing — in NH, she has at times risen to fifth place out of a still-crowded Democratic primary of 18 candidates. She has also outlasted formerly top-tier candidates like Beto O'Rourke and, in NH, is outpolling candidates who have out-raised her.

For instance, Gabbard is passing up Kamala Harris, whose poll numbers crashed soon after the July debate in which Gabbard lashed out at her record as a prosecuting attorney. The Hawaiian congresswoman has only raised a quarter of the USD 36 million the Californian senator has pocketed. Yet Harris, the only Indian-American candidate, is not only sinking in the polls but has failed to galvanize Indian diaspora support. As *India Abroad* reported in April, Indian-American donations to Gabbard surpassed those to Harris by a margin of more than three to one.

Gabbard is making significant strides as she demonstrates a willingness to go head-to-head with her own party's establishment.

During the 2016 presidential election, Clinton was widely perceived as "untrustworthy' and "unethical," a perception that Gabbard plays upon. On the eve of the 20 November Democratic debate, Gabbard's attorneys accused Clinton of defamation, demanding she retract her 17 October description of the congresswoman as the "favorite of the Russians."

Gabbard's demand has some standing. On 24 October, Fairness & Accuracy In Reporting — a national media watch group — rubbished the allegations. "There is no evidence that Gabbard... is any kind of Russian agent," reported FAIR. Such "silly accusations," the group stated, are rather a nonsensical distraction from "the reality that Gabbard's most troubling attribute is her documented connection to the far-right Hindu nationalist, or Hindutva, movement known as Rashtriya Swayamsevak Sangh (RSS), the parent organization of India's ruling BJP party."

That connection traces back to 2011, a year before Gabbard was first elected to the US Congress and long before the BJP rose to power in India.

As she sought election and then re-election, Gabbard owed much of her success to support from the same leaders of overseas wings of the RSS and BJP who mobilized to get Modi into office. Even as evidence of this connection emerged over the past year, her campaign has entrenched her notoriously close relationship with Modi while reciting RSS/BJP talking points in defense of the Hindu nationalist movement.

Gabbard made a name for herself among American progressives in 2016 when she resigned from her powerful position on the Democratic National Committee to endorse socialist Bernie Sanders for president — a move that put her at odds with then Democratic front-runner Clinton. Today, however, she is at odds with Sanders not only as his opponent in the 2020 Democratic primary but on foreign policy issues. One conspicuous example is their contrasting positions on Kashmir.

"I am also deeply concerned about the situation in Kashmir," said Sanders on 31 August 2019 — just three weeks after the abrogation of Article 370. Criticizing the "communications blackout" and "crackdown in the name of 'security'," he declared, "India's action is unacceptable."

"It is complex," said Gabbard when asked about Kashmir at an 8 September campaign rally. Referring to the 1990 exodus of Kashmiri Pandits, she said, "Many families were driven from their homes there, and fled, and have not been able to return home." Insisting that Kashmiri women previously had no rights to own property, she added, "The previous government had policies in place that made homosexuality illegal."

Her rhetoric directly mirrored that of India's right-wing which, as journalist Anish Gawande explained, increasingly adopts the argument that "Article 370 was removed to protect minorities."

The result is that LGBTQ rights are "used as bait to

target every voice decrying the changes to Article 370." This tactic was forcefully employed in October, for instance, when masked protestors, shouting "Gay for J&K," shut down a London University panel on Kashmir.

None of the other Democratic presidential candidates have echoed Gabbard's BJP-esque rhetoric.

"I'm really concerned about what's happened in Kashmir," said O'Rourke in mid-September (before he dropped out). Elizabeth Warren, currently a front-runner, recently remarked, "The rights of the people of Kashmir must be respected." Even Harris warned that "we are all watching" and referred to the possible need to intervene to prevent any human rights abuses.

Gabbard's interest in swimming against the progressive current was further illustrated by her response to Modi's recent visit to the US.

The 'Howdy Modi' rockstar reception on 22 September in Houston, Texas was supposed to be a propaganda bonanza for the BJP. As ANI reported, BJP Foreign Affairs Cell In-Charge, Vijay Chauthaiwale, "spearheaded the preparations." Over 60 "prominent US lawmakers, including... Tulsi Gabbard" were slated to attend, reported *India Today*.

The event ended in disarray. Ultimately, only 21 US congressional representatives attended. Only one of five Indian-American lawmakers — Congressman Raja Krishnamoorthi — showed up.

Even Gabbard herself was a no-show, although her exit was clouded by confusion. Reports circulated that she dropped out in solidarity with fellow Hindu-American Congressman Ro Khanna's recent call to "reject Hindutva" — yet, reported *DNA India*, she "vehemently denied the claims." India's ambassador to the US, Harsh Shringla, rushed to her defense, calling her a "staunch supporter" of Modi. Issuing a welcome video, she apologized for missing Modi's rockstar reception "due to previously scheduled presidential campaign events." She added that a strong partnership with India can "bring about the ideal of *Vasudhaiva Kutumbakam*" — a phrase (meaning "the world is one family") which professor Audrey Truschke noted has been adopted by Hindutva groups such as the Vishwa Hindu Parishad.

Of the 65,000 people present at "Howdy Modi," an estimated 15,000 were protestors outside the event. Yet Gabbard stated the event was "bringing together Indian-Americans and Hindu-Americans from across our country." Then she met Modi on 27 September in New York City.

It was their fifth meeting in five years.

As Gabbard met Modi, Truschke and others were outside protesting. "Modi and his political party, the BJP, openly adhere to Hindutva," declared Truschke at the protest. "The Modi *sarkar* [regime] has made it very clear that all who oppose Hindutva are enemies. Really, anyone who merely accurately describes Hindutva is an enemy in the eyes of the Modi government. As a result, the BJP and associated groups have ruthlessly attacked the media, academics, and any other dissenters in India."

Yet Gabbard was unfazed.

That weekend, her campaign launched a new fundraiser — a raffle for a free trip to India. Featuring a photo of her garlanding Modi, the fundraiser was hosted at the (now defunct) URL: tulsi2020.com/Howdy.

In a 13 October interview with Gabbard, *The Times of India*, noting that she had missed 'Howdy Modi', asked, "How do you view such rallies and the expression of what some people see as an upsurge of Hindu nationalism and

Hindu pride?" She responded: "Hindu nationalism is a term that many people are using frequently without being specific about what they mean by that. Why is expressing pride in one's religion a bad thing?"

Gabbard further asked, "If you take out the word Hindu and you replace it with Muslim or Catholic or Jewish, then what do you end up with?" The answer is, of course, you end up with religious nationalism no matter which religious label precedes the "nationalism" term.

Tulsi Gabbard is not the only Democratic presidential candidate with links to India's far-right — though she is apparently the only one offering apologetics for Hindutva and its alleged atrocities.

"Links to Modi and Hindu nationalism can even be found in at least three Democratic presidential campaigns," wrote journalist Rashmee Kumar. She cited frontrunner Joe Biden, whose campaign recently hired the son of the Overseas Friends of the BJP (OFBJP) co-founder and Pete Buttigieg, whose campaign policy director is the former national coordinator of VHP-America and daughter of a former OFBJP vice-president.

Nor is Gabbard the only US congressional representative associated with the RSS.

Raja Krishnamoorthi joined RSS Chief Mohan Bhagwat at last year's World Hindu Congress in Chicago — an event Gabbard, after months of pressure, eventually publicly dropped out of — and recently headlined a celebration of the RSS's founding organized by the group's international wing, the Hindu Swayamsevak Sangh.

FAIR reported, Gabbard has "received crucial financial support from the Indian-American far right." Her funding from RSS-affiliated donors traces back to before she was first elected in November 2012. In 2013, approximately 21 percent of her donations came from members and executives of Hindutva groups — rising to approximately 24 percent in her second year in office.

While Clinton levels allegations that incite American political commentators to rant about Gabbard's perceived support from Russia, they overlook the real hard evidence that her actual support comes from — and goes to — India's Hindu nationalist movement.

In late October 2019, Gabbard announced that she won't seek re-election to US Congress. "I've always done my best to serve where I felt I could make the most impact," she declared. "I believe I can best serve the people of Hawaii and our country as your President."

Gabbard has found her niche as the anti-establishment and anti-war candidate.

"I'm running for president to rebuild our Democratic party, take it out of the hands of the foreign policy establishment in Washington, the military industrial complex, and greedy corporate interests and truly put it in the hands of the people," she declared at the 20 November debate. Cashing in on her military service, she added, "I volunteered to deploy to Iraq where every single day I saw the terribly high human cost of war. No, I'm not going to put party interest first. I will put the interest of the American people above all else."

Her rhetoric is reminiscent of Donald Trump's "drain the swamp" slogan. It's a populist, anti-corruption, proletariat vs bourgeoisie message. Perhaps then it's not surprising that Gabbard's support base overlaps with Trump's — as one analysis of poll respondents revealed, her supporters "are more likely to have backed President Trump in 2016, hold conservative views or identify as Republican compared to voters backing the other candidates." Her no-holds-barred brawl with Clinton — who, as the 2016 Democratic nominee, was the subject of "lock her up" chants at Trump campaign rallies — has certainly won her fans on the Right. Even Trump's campaign has applauded her criticism of her own party.

Tulsi Gabbard is in an all-or-nothing campaign for president.

She is rising in the polls and remains standing as others who once appeared strong fall by the wayside. She faces long odds to secure the nomination, but that was also once true of Donald Trump.

Whatever comes to pass, since she appears certain to stay in the presidential race at least until July 2020, her association with the international Hindutva movement deserves deeper scrutiny.

Originally published by The Quint [TheQuint.com].

— 11 —
The Princess of the RSS and Me

27 July 2020

I was in New Delhi when it all started.

It was August 2018. For several months, I'd been aware of US Congresswoman Tulsi Gabbard's strange intimacy with India's ruling Bharatiya Janata Party and her effusive praise of BJP Prime Minister Narendra Modi, whom she called "a leader whose example and dedication to the people he serves should be an inspiration to elected officials everywhere." It was an odd accolade for an American politician to give a pogrom-tainted Indian politician, but I quickly glossed over it as the natural fawning of a co-chair of the House India Caucus.

I was enjoying exploring the ruins of Tughlaqabad Fort, Jahaz Mahal, and Begampura Masjid — all while planning an excursion to Goa — so I didn't give it much more thought at the time.

Then someone sent me a picture of Tulsi Gabbard wearing a BJP scarf while posing with the former head of the BJP's Foreign Affairs Cell. And then I learned that Gabbard was intended to chair the World Hindu Congress in Chicago, a co-production of the violent Hindu nationalist Vishwa Hindu Parishad (which the CIA had just named as a "religious militant organization) and the group's US affiliate, VHP-America. The WHC's scheduled keynote was Mohan Bhagwat, head of the Rashtriya Swayamsevak Sangh, the mothership of Hindu nationalism.

Around the same time, some of Gabbard's constituents in Hawaii began contacting me to express concern about her association with Hindu nationalist organizations. They alleged that she had received hundreds of thousands of dollars in donations from US-based members of those groups. I asked for more information but, reluctant to expose themselves, they declined to share it.

So I started digging.

It only took me a few hours of researching Gabbard's congressional campaign donations on the Federal Election Commission website to discover that some of her earliest top-dollar donors — before she was first elected — included people like Ramesh Bhutada (Vice-President of Hindu Swayamsevak Sangh, the international wing of the RSS), his cousin-in-law Vijay Pallod (HSS and VHPA), Mihir Meghani (HSS and VHPA), Chandrakant Patel (President of the Overseas Friends of the BJP), and a host of other executives from HSS, VHPA, OFBJP, and affiliated groups.

Along the way, I discovered that Gabbard had invited RSS spokesperson Ram Madhav to her wedding in 2015.

Soon after, I was invited for an interview with a Hawaiian radio show. "Gabbard is spending her time working as hard as possible to bring the Hindu nationalist agenda to American soil," I told the host. Speaking from a sweltering, sticky, mid-monsoon New Delhi, I continued, "Her stance is not only empowering extremists in India to continue engaging in violence against ethnic minorities there, but she's also using her political platform to deliberately conceal the reality of the situation for Indian minorities, as well as to help to bring Hindu nationalist figures who promote violence — such as the head of the RSS, Mohan Bhagwat."

A few days later, when a coalition of 11 South Asian organizations released a letter calling on Gabbard to disavow her ties to Hindu nationalist groups, I was asked to comment.

"The RSS is India's version of the KKK," I said. "They press an agenda of Hindu supremacy which is practically indistinguishable from white nationalism. Unfortunately, the RSS has gained far more ground in India than the KKK has in the United States. Sangh Parivar groups preach that India is, and always has been, a Hindu nation for Hindu people and that non-Hindus don't belong in the country unless they glorify Hinduism. Bhagwat's comments over the past several years reveal that he advances this exact ideology. Appearing alongside Bhagwat is comparable to taking the stage with David Duke."

Finally, in September 2018, just days before the WHC began in Chicago, Gabbard released a statement disassociating herself from it. "Due to ethical concerns and problems that surround my participating in any partisan Indian political event in America, effective immediately, I respectfully withdraw myself from serving as Honorary Chair of the World Hindu Congress 2018," she said.

I wasn't satisfied, however. "This is too little and too late from Tulsi Gabbard," I said. "She is trying to back-paddle out of choppy waters only after it became too politically inexpedient to keep surfing the Hindutva wave of hate. Gabbard's political career exists because of financing and promotion provided by US-based affiliates of the RSS and VHP. She has spent the past five years serving as the handmaiden of Hindutva…. It's great that Gabbard issued this statement, and hopefully it throws a monkey wrench into the gears of the WHC, but she certainly did it because of external pressure rather than true principles."

So I set out to document, in pain-staking detail, exactly how Gabbard was funded by Hindutva groups, who gave, when they gave, where they gave, and, most importantly, why they gave.

It was a snowy January of 2019 in Zagreb, Croatia. Gabbard had just announced her campaign for president. I had holed up in an Airbnb in a high-rise apartment in the suburbs to research and write for weeks.

As I pieced the story together — tracking down HSS or VHPA events Gabbard had attended, identifying OFBJP leaders who donated to her, and locating videos where Hindu nationalists praised her for supporting Modi before his election — a friend reached out to me. "We need to do something about Tulsi Gabbard," she said. "Somebody has to write something." I agreed, asking, "What if I've already written something?" That's when she put me in touch with *Caravan* magazine. Soon after, they commissioned the article for publication.

Soon after, someone contacted me with a crucial piece of the puzzle. They had the name of the person who originally put Gabbard in touch with the RSS. Michael Brannon Parker, a former resident of Hawaii, who had worked for the RSS's Ram Madhav.

By March 2019, I'd returned to my native California, where I got wind that acquaintances in the South Asian diaspora were planning to protest Gabbard at one of her presidential town hall events in Los Angeles. I also learned there would an open mic for the audience to ask her questions. It was too good of an opportunity for me to pass up, so I showed up — arriving early, sitting near the front and, aware that my negative remarks about her over the past several months might make me too easily identifiable if I wore my distinctive leather flat cap, wearing a baseball cap and eyeglasses.

After she spoke, they began taking audience questions. My hopes dropped for a moment when emcee Jimmy Dore

— a comedian turned political commentator — announced that they would only take three questions. Armed with a written question, I shot my hand up anyways and was shocked when Dore pointed at me first. "Let's take this gentleman right here in the hat," he said. I stood, greeted Gabbard with an "aloha," and removed my hat and glasses.

"He's taking the hat and glasses off now," said Gabbard. "It's getting serious." It was indeed.

"Hawaii resident Michael Brannon Parker says he has known you since you were a child and he introduced you to the RSS, a violent paramilitary in India," I said. As she began to scowl, I continued: "Vijay Pallod of Texas is a leader in RSS-affiliated groups in the USA, and he confirms that he met you through Michael Brannon Parker. In you first two terms in office, you also met the RSS spokesperson at least three times. And you spoke at many RSS events, including two in India. When did your collaboration with the RSS and how much money have they given you?"

Gabbard paused for several seconds before answering, then declared, "I'm a soldier, and I took an oath. One oath in my life. That was an oath to serve and protect this country. To put my life on the line for the people of this country. We stand for aloha. We stand for diversity. We stand for peace and bringing people together around these shared ideals of freedom and opportunity for all people…. It is this kind of attacks that are rooted in religious bigotry."

She completely side-stepped the content of the question, of course, something she would continue to do as the issue arose again and again over the next year of her presidential campaign.

By then, I had identified over 50 executives in US-based Sangh groups (HSS, VHPA, OFBJP, etc) who began donating to Gabbard in her first two terms (2011–2014, leading up to Modi's election in India), approximately 200 donors identifiable as active members of such groups, and about ten different Sangh events which she had attended. It was more than enough to confirm my thesis that Gabbard's congressional career was financed by US affiliates of India's ruling party. And yet I wanted to compare notes with someone else — just to make sure.

Encouraged by *Caravan* to get into the field, I flew to Hawaii in April 2019. It was my first time in the Aloha State. Landing in Maui, I rented a room from a Jewish chiropractor in his 70s who had emigrated from New Jersey. My days I spent meeting with a constituent of Gabbard who had researched her financial links with the American Sangh. It must have taken her years, but she had compiled meticulously organized and color-coded databases of donations. As I swilled black coffee, we corroborated names, Sangh affiliations, dates, and amounts. Everything matched — the only difference was that she had dug up a bit more than even I had.

I flew from Maui to the "Big Island" to attend the Hawaii County Democratic Party Convention, where I met and interviewed State Senator Kai Kahele, who had recently stepped forward to challenge Gabbard for her seat in Congress. Waking at 5am in a hotel in Kona, I was picked up by a local who drove me across the island to Honokaa, stopping along the way for eggs, donuts, and coffee. After a long, rainy day spent inside the convention, I flew back to Maui in the evening. The next morning, I sat on the porch of my host, palm trees swaying in the breeze behind me, and reported:

> I have made strong allegations about how her

congressional career was financed, from the earliest days, by American affiliates of India's fascist paramilitary organization, the RSS.

My fieldwork in Hawaii not only confirms this, but suggests that the extent of Gabbard's ties to this violent paramilitary group are far deeper than even my own independent research has already established.

But I also discovered that a large segment of her constituents are disturbed by the congresswoman for another reason.

Yesterday, I was at the Hawaii County Democratic Party Convention in Honokaa on the Big Island. Over 200 people attended the all-day event. Several state senators and state representatives were there. The Lieutenant Governor even attended. One man, a local from Honokaa, told me that Gabbard was also invited. Showing no interest in interacting with her constituents, however, she refused to attend.

Instead, she was in Los Angeles campaigning for president. She showed up to do a photo-op for a park clean-up — in LA. Gabbard billed it as a "service before self" event. But a lot of her Hawaiian constituents seem to feel that it was more of a "presidential ambitions before congressional representation" event.

They think that Gabbard is a power-hungry politician who is never in her district to care for and represent her own constituents.

Why is Tulsi Gabbard so ambitious? What is the driving force behind her ambitions? If not her constituents, then who does she really represent?

I've always remembered my father's account of his visit to Hawaii. He said that it's an incredible place with an unbelievably beautiful climate, but that it takes two weeks to acclimatize. As I came to the end of my week-long visit, the heat and humidity had given me a sore throat and I was losing my voice. I spent my last day there in bed as my host made me herbal tea. We chatted about Judaism and oddball families as he prepared to depart for New Jersey to join his family for Passover celebrations and I prepared to return to California — and from there to the Netherlands — to complete my composition.

My editor, Puja Sen, told me that journalistic integrity required I at least attempt to contact some of the Sangh members mentioned in my article. I was reluctant to do so, but when I finally bit the bullet and started making calls, I was surprised that several of them were willing to talk at length. I secured several fascinating interviews, including with Vijay Pallod — the first Sangh leader to donate to Gabbard — who disclosed his family's intimacy with RSS Chief Mohan Bhagwat.

The calls, however, soon provoked the first smear article against me. When I called Mihir Meghani, he declined to answer questions over the phone — or schedule a time to do so — and insisted I email the questions instead. He never responded. Instead, on 28 July, three days before *Caravan* went to print with my article, Meghani's organization, Hindu American Foundation, published a letter to the magazine in which they accused me of, among other things, "verbally harassing Hindu American children and their parents," stated (without evidence) that I have claimed that Gandhi "allied himself with Adolf Hitler" (which I have not), and described me as "an activist who not only associates with, but promotes the ideology of those who espouse violent separatism in India" (which is nonsense).

Shoot the messenger, thus, was the strategy. It didn't matter what I was reporting. It only mattered who I was — or, more accurately, accused of being.

Nevertheless, while I was on vacation in France near the city of Toulouse, my article was published. Ashok Swain, a professor at Uppsala University in Sweden said it revealed how Gabbard was "being promoted by India's Hindu Supremacists." Richard Fox Young, a professor at Princeton Theological Seminary, called it "a deep probe." Journalist Anjali Kamat described it as "a timely reminder of Gabbard's deep ties to the diaspora Hindu right." And then Congressman Ro Khanna took notice.

It was a hot August day and I was relaxing on a bench on the banks of Lake Zurich — hours after speaking at a rally in support of freedom in Kashmir — when I checked my Twitter account to discover that Khanna, one of only five Indian-American in US Congress, had replied to my posting of the article. Publicly, he wrote, "Important article. It's the duty of every American politician of Hindu faith to stand for pluralism, reject Hindutva, and speak for equal rights for Hindus, Muslims, Sikhs, Buddhist & Christians." Privately, he messaged me, writing, "Fascinating article. I have been quite critical of Modi and haven't met him since being elected. I also got extraordinary heat recently for joining the Pakistan caucus. How we navigate the issue of right wing nationalism is the challenge of our time. Thanks for your article."

Not everyone expressed the same gratitude. The day before, on 28 August, diaspora newspaper *India Herald* reported on the "elaborate hit piece on Tulsi Gabbard's presidential bid" that painted Gabbard as a "nominee of the right wing Hindu nationalists." Vinod Prakash, the founder of RSS-linked India Development and Relief Fund wrote described it as "a glaring example of malicious journalism" and insisted my mention of IDRF was "based solely on the smear campaign against us led by avowed Left/Marxist anti-Hindu forces."

Sacramento attorney Amar Shergill, however, believed that Khanna's comments about my article represented a "seismic shift in Indo-centric politics." Declaring that "Khanna's statement breaks new ground for South Asians and for all in the progressive movement," he praised the congressman for having "stated in decisive moral terms that the dominant political ideology of India must be rejected as a matter of fundamental human rights." Shergill concluded:

> The full measure of Khanna's words is yet to be felt. Modi and the Indian government are certain to be dismayed by this challenge to the inroads they have made within certain sectors of the Indian community in the US.
>
> In the coming months, we will see a debate within the South Asian American community and the Democratic Party regarding the morality of Hindutva and how the party can reach consensus given the political crisis in India. Khanna's statement goes to the heart of this debate by laying bare the obvious hypocrisy of Hindutva's American supporters.
>
> South Asian Americans simply cannot claim to support civil rights and equality for all Americans while simultaneously advocating for religious supremacy that results in the rape, torture, murder

and oppression of minorities in India.

About two weeks later, Terrence McNulty — a writer of unknown screenplays — denounced my article as "a smear piece," claiming, "Pieter Friedrich has his own political agenda and sees Tulsi Gabbard as a convenient conduit through which to raise awareness of his cause." Two weeks after that, Dr. Ramesh Rao — a professor at Columbus State University who had previously described me, during my protests against the WHC, as a "rabble-rouser" — announced that Khanna's affirmation of the importance of my article represented support for "the terrorist-affiliated Pieter Friedrich." A week after that, the HSS itself staged a protest against Khanna — or, more accurately, against me.

At a 3 October town hall for Khanna's constituents, approximately 25 members of HSS stood outside holding placards bearing my picture alongside slogans accusing him of siding with "bigots." Inside the event, Khanna was quizzed about why he tweeted in response to my article, to which he answered: "I responded to one of his articles saying that I believe in pluralism. There were a few groups in the community who got offended by that. I have no tolerance for right wing nationalists who are affiliating with Trump. And let me tell you something — they're in an echo chamber, but their bigotry, their right wing nationalism, their support for Trump or for white supremacy is a minority. But they will see that our district is pluralistic and I have no problem standing up against them."

Meanwhile, Gabbard — who was on the campaign trail — kept violating the first law of holes: if you find yourself in one, stop digging.

At a 1 October town hall for her campaign in New Hampshire, an audience member challenged her about her support for Modi. Specifically, they mentioned Modi's orchestration of the 2002 Gujarat Pogrom. Gabbard shot back: "Do you know what instigated those riots?"

"Imagine someone saying that about *Kristallnacht*, the first Nazi pogrom against the Jews," I noted in response — a reference to the fact that the assassination of a German diplomat in Paris by a Jewish teenager was used by the Nazis as an excuse to stage the pogrom. Gabbard continued digging, however. "Hindu nationalism is a term that many people are using frequently without being specific about what they mean by that," she said in a 13 October interview "Why is expressing pride in one's religion a bad thing?"

Why, indeed, should mingling religion with nationalism be considered problematic? That's a rhetorical question.

Meanwhile, Jimmy Dore — the erstwhile comedian who was, no doubt, bitter about picking me to ask Gabbard a question at her town hall earlier that year — interviewed Khanna. "That guy Friedrich, you know, he's not a real writer," said Dore in the 3 October interview. "You know that he has sketchy background, he's an activist involved with a terrorist organization."

Dore's last-ditch effort to bolster Gabbard's failing political aspirations by defaming me were destined to fail.

On 24 October, less than a week after I celebrated my birthday on the Seine in Paris, Fairness & Accuracy in Reporting reported, "Gabbard's most troubling attribute is her documented connection to the far-right Hindu nationalist, or Hindutva, movement known as Rashtriya Swayamsevak Sangh (RSS), the parent organization of India's ruling BJP party." Describing my article as "the best chronicle of her affiliation with the Indian right," the watchdog group explained, "The RSS draws much of its power from its followers in the Diaspora, and Gabbard has been crucial to revamping the image of the Hindu nationalist in the United States, and has in turn received crucial financial support from the Indian-American far right."

The next day, Gabbard announced she would not seek re-election to US Congress.

She continued her campaign for the presidency, however. Entrenching herself in New Hampshire, the first state in the country to hold presidential primaries, she invested everything she had in a strong performance in that election. Not ready to retire the issue until Gabbard herself shuttered all of her electoral campaigns, however, I decided to fly to New Hampshire and make a little bit of noise.

On 6 January 2020, speaking at the city council meeting of Londonderry — the city where Gabbard had asked about what instigated the riots in response to a question about her whitewashing Modi's orchestration of the 2002 Gujarat Pogrom — I referenced her keynote speech at an OFBJP in 2014, stating, "The BJP's Foreign Affairs Cell Chief discussed her campaign for re-election to a second term. The foreign politician told the American congresswoman: 'Your victory later this year is a foregone conclusion.' Then Gabbard posed for pictures wearing a scarf with the BJP logo."

My remarks followed a 5 January town hall by Gabbard at which my friend, Jada Bernard, quizzed her about why she had worn the BJP scarf, to which she replied: "Sometimes, as we're standing ... people come up and they want to take a picture. Somebody put something around my neck and snapped a picture without my knowing what it was."

Two days later, I attended a Gabbard town hall at which she was scheduled to appear — but backed out last minute upon announcing that she had to return to Washington, DC for crucial votes. As the organizers conducted a virtual interview with the congresswoman, I and others unfurled signs regarding her affiliation with India's Hindu nationalist movement. As I hoisted a sign reading "Tulsi whitewashes India's KKK," her staffers — including her Deputy National Campaign Director — charged me, grabbed me, pushed me, shoved me, and hustled me out of the room.

Hindutva's handmaiden had fallen. The princess of the RSS had lost her crown. And the figurehead of Hindu nationalism in America had failed at her absurd attempt to obtain the presidency.

Originally published by the author on Medium.com.

— 12 —
Looming Threat of Genocide in India

29 February 2020

Last month, a widowed Muslim woman in India was arrested and charged with sedition — that is, with inciting an insurrection.

Here's the background. India's Hindu nationalist government wants to pass a law requiring that every resident of the country prove their citizenship.

In the state of Karnataka, this proposed National Register of Citizens was the subject of a school play which portrayed a worried family discussing their fears about how the NRC could be used to strip Muslims of citizenship.

The ten-year-old daughter of the detained widow, acting in the play, delivered a line about how she would use her shoes to beat anyone who demanded that she prove her citizenship.

The child's brief dialogue caused a national scandal.

Police accused the girl of "insulting" the prime minister. They arrested her widowed mother as well as the school's headmistress. And they visited the school at least five times to gather evidence and interrogate the students about the play.

A month earlier, another school play in Karnataka received a very different reaction.

While ministers from the Central and State governments sat in the audience, child actors surged onto the stage to re-enact the mob destruction of the Babri mosque while an off-screen narrator praised them for "demolishing the structure" with anything they could get their hands on. Later, the school's director — a member of the Rashtriya Swayamsevak Sangh, a Hindu nationalist paramilitary — defended the play, arguing that it taught children how to "live for the country" and showed them how to "remove insults to the nation."

Police only acted after demands by a third-party prompted them to file minor charges against the school's administration — but, according to the complainant, they "have not bothered to proceed with the investigation."

The 16th-century Babri mosque, built in the city of Ayodhya in the state of Uttar Pradesh, stood on a site that Hindu nationalists insist is the location where the Hindu deity Ram was born.

After affiliates of the RSS paramilitary launched a campaign to remove the mosque, the Bharatiya Janata Party officially joined the movement. While the president of the BJP toured the country to promote the campaign, an RSS worker named Narendra Modi worked behind the scenes, pulling the strings as he took responsibility for logistics, crowd mobilization, and other arrangements.

The campaign culminated in December 1992 as hundreds of thousands rallied around the mosque to listen to speeches by BJP leaders — sparked by their fiery rhetoric, the mob surged forward and destroyed the mosque.

The destruction was followed by pogroms throughout northern India which left up to 3,000 Muslims dead.

The destruction represented what international relations expert Dibyesh Anand calls a "poetics of fear" where "minority Muslims have no option but to accept their subjugation or face further violence" — but it was also, in the words of sociologist Prema Kurien, "a watershed event in the history of the Hindu nationalist movement" which "propelled the BJP... into the limelight." According to

Human Rights Watch, the violence "helped catapult the BJP into power in the early 1990s."

That's how the BJP always rises to power. On the blood of the innocent. On a wave of hatred manifested in vicious atrocities that are always met with impunity and in which the perpetrators are invariably punished with promotion to ever higher positions of power.

The BJP still held national power in 2002 when Modi was elected chief minister of the state of Gujarat.

Three days later, the state was the site of India's first and worst pogrom of the 21st century.

Commanded by BJP politicians and RSS leaders, and joined by the police, mobs ran rampage across Gujarat for three days, slaughtering Muslim men, women, and children, raping them, dismembering them, burning them alive. Leaders of the pogrom later bragged that Modi sanctioned their violence, ordered police to allow the massacre, and told the killers that they could have free reign to do whatever they wanted for three days. At the end of those three days, 2,000 — or more — lay dead.

That's how Modi earned the nickname "The Butcher of Gujarat."

Modi was complicit — but he was never charged. A state minister from his own party blew the whistle, and then he was assassinated. A senior police officer also blew the whistle, and then he was fired and later arrested on trumped up charges. Modi was banned from entering the US and the UK, but then he became Prime Minister of India and is now greeted with open arms.

Since Modi rose to power as the Butcher of Gujarat, it was no secret how he would govern India nor should it be any surprise that his administration is now marked by extreme violence. Nor should we be shocked that India is on the brink of genocide — the only surprising thing is that it hasn't happened yet.

Every major action the BJP has taken over the past year has brought India exponentially closer to the edge of catastrophic violence.

In 2019, Modi's regime scrapped the constitutional article that had granted the state of Jammu and Kashmir semi-autonomous status for over 70 years. Then he ramped up the troop presence and put the entire region on lockdown — where it remains. Kashmir has remained cut off from the rest of the world — a complete black zone — for over six months.

Modi's regime passed the Ayodhya verdict, giving the same violent Hindu nationalists who destroyed the Babri mosque permission to build a temple on the site. His government is now entrusted with ensuring construction of the temple. Thus, the BJP, discarding all semblance of secularism, entered the temple-building business.

Modi's regime passed the Citizenship Amendment Act, providing undocumented immigrants a fast-track to citizenship — as long as they're not Muslim. The CAA marks the first time in the history of the Republic of India that religion has been made the criteria for citizenship. The CAA also serves a crucial role when partnered with the proposed National Register of Citizens.

Modi's regime, which already implemented the NRC in the state of Assam last year, now wants to impose it nationwide. That would require that every resident of the country prove their citizenship. That's a scary idea for every Indian — but it's truly terrifying for Muslims because of how the CAA and the NRC are designed to work in sync with each other.

The NRC would require that every Indian resident

prove they are a citizen, but the CAA is the loophole allowing any non-Muslim who cannot do so to remain in the country and get on a fast-track to normalizing their status and securing their citizenship. Muslims, on the other hand, have no loophole. Even if they are citizens, if they can't prove it, they potentially face being sent to a detention center and... God only knows what from there on.

A legal method for cleansing the country of Muslims is exactly what the BJP intended the CAA and the NRC to provide.

And they've made no secret of it.

Amit Shah — president of the BJP, Home Minister of India, and the man responsible for pushing through the CAA — has declared that all Hindus, Sikhs, Buddhists, and Christians will get citizenship whether they can prove they are citizens or not. Clarifying that the CAA is intended as a loophole to enable the government to target Muslims while putting no one else at risk, he says that it was brought in "exactly" to ensure that no non-Muslims lose their citizenship. When the NRC comes in after the CAA, he says, undocumented immigrants need not worry "but infiltrators should."

Infiltrators. Shah loves that term. "Every infiltrator will be thrown out of the country," he has promised. They will be thrown out "one by one" and "no infiltrator will be allowed to stay." Shah pledges to ensure "a nationwide identification of illegal infiltrators living in the country" and vows that, once the NRC is conducted across India, "each and every infiltrator [will be] identified and expelled."

Termites. That's another term Shah loves. "Infiltrators are like termites in the soil," he declares. "The illegal immigrants are like termites."

Lest there be any confusion which people — or which community — Shah means when he speaks of "infiltrators" and "termites," his fellow party leaders have spoken to remove any ambiguity.

A virus. That's what the BJP's Yogi Adityanath, the Chief Minister of Uttar Pradesh, calls Muslims. A "green virus" — green being identified as the color of Islam — which has "infected" the opposition. "Muslims did no favor to India by staying here," he says. Nor will they stay, if he has anything to do about it.

As protests against the CAA and the NRC have swept across India, Modi's regime has met the largely peaceful protestors with brute force. Until recently, Uttar Pradesh was the epicenter of the government's violent attempts to stamp out the resistance.

Since December 2019, over 20 people have died in UP's anti-CAA protests. Countless videos show masses of peaceful protestors breaking like waves on the rocks as police charge them and begin randomly brutalizing people. Sanctioning the unprovoked attacks, Chief Minister Adityanath has even vowed to "take revenge" against protestors.

The BJP leader's "revenge" has manifested in targeted violence against Muslims throughout the state.

In one instance, a 73-year-old Muslim attorney was arrested and taken to a police station in the dead of night. While they beat him in custody, police threatened to destroy his family, throw them all in jail "where they will rot for life," and rape his mother. The many other allegations of atrocities include claims that Muslim teenagers are being picked up by police and subjected to emotional, psychological, and physical torture for hours or days on end.

Police are also accused of breaking into mosques, schools, and homes to terrorize Muslim families. In the midnight hours, they appear at Muslim homes to threaten women and children unless they disclose the location of the male members of the family. Forcing their way in, they ransack houses, splintering the furniture, and stealing valuables. Along the way, they vandalize cars and smash security cameras to erase evidence of their crimes.

Universities — strongholds for pluralistic protests against the CAA and the NRC — are also under attack.

At Aligarh Muslim University, police laid siege to the campus, calling the students "terrorists" and chanting "Jai Shri Ram" — a slogan meaning "Hail Lord Ram" which Hindu nationalists have adopted as a war cry.

The violence mirrored that at Jamia Millia Islamia, a university in Delhi. Invading the campus, police fired tear gas into the library, then entered to begin trashing the rooms as they randomly thrashed traumatized students.

At the height of this unchecked violence, a national cabinet minister poured fuel on the fire.

In late January, as Finance Minister Anurag Thakur spoke at a BJP rally, he led the crowd in chants of "shoot the traitors" — a slogan that was previously raised by masked members of the RSS's student wing as they ran rampage across the Jawaharlal Nehru University campus in Delhi, screaming "Jai Shri Ram" while they attacked students with iron rods, bricks, and acid.

Who, exactly, are the "traitors"?

The traitors are anti-CAA protestors — but, more specifically, they are any non-Hindus living in India. That much was made obvious when, as several people acted on the call to "shoot the traitors" by opening fire on anti-CAA protests, one of the shooters shouted: "In our country, only Hindus will prevail."

That's the goal of Hindutva.

Hindutva is the religious nationalist political ideology that claims India is a country of Hindus, for Hindus, and only for Hindus and that anyone who is not a Hindu is a foreigner, an internal threat, and a traitor.

Hindutva is the guiding ideology of the RSS.

Founded in 1925, the RSS is the oldest and largest non-governmental paramilitary organization in the world. It is all-male, uniformed, and armed. It developed in parallel with European fascist movements like those in Mussolini's Italy and Hitler's Germany. It took ideological inspiration from — and even engaged in direct contact with — Europe's fascists. And it is responsible for at least a dozen pogroms since India achieved independence in 1947.

In 1925, Hitler published *Mein Kampf* and founded the Schutzstaffel, or SS, the organization responsible for the Holocaust; meanwhile, in India, Hindu nationalists founded the RSS.

The RSS's founders claimed that "we are Indians because we are Hindus" and that "Indian patriotism" is synonymous with "Hindu patriotism."

They insisted that the subcontinent should actually be called "Hindustan" because it is a "a nation of Hindu people" just like a "Germany of Germans."

Looking to Western fascists for inspiration, the man who mentored the first Supreme Leader of the RSS traveled to Italy to meet Mussolini.

Upon meeting the Italian dictator, he praised "the idea of fascism" for bringing out the "conception of unity amongst people." Applauding the fascist youth organizations in both Italy and Germany, he called them necessary and "eminently suited for introduction in India," insisted that Hindu nationalists should imitate them, and declared that "our institution of [the] RSS... is of this kind."

Meanwhile, the Nazis came to power in Germany, Hitler was made dictator, and the first concentration camp was constructed.

Soon, they began laying the groundwork for the Holocaust as they passed the Nuremberg Laws and then staged the first pogrom against the Jews. While *Kristallnacht* left 100 Jews dead as tens of thousands more were deported to concentration camps, the RSS's ideologues argued that their concept of a Hindu nation was justified by the dominance of the racial majority in Nazi Germany.

The ideologues warned that Indian Muslims may have to "play the part of German Jews," even as the RSS's founders complained that "the Muslims are making themselves a nuisance," claimed that "we shall have to fight" them, and suggested that, for that purpose, "The RSS may be useful and handy."

While the Nazis sparked the Second World War with the invasion of Poland, the second and longest-serving Supreme Leader of the RSS published his manifesto as the "first systematic statement of RSS ideology."

Today, Golwalkar is revered as the Guru of the RSS. In 1939, the year that he published his manifesto, he was already second-in-command of the paramilitary. A year later, he became chief of the RSS, a post he held until his death in 1973.

"In Hindustan, the land of the Hindus, lives and should live the Hindu nation," he wrote. "Only the Hindu has been living here as the child of this soil."

He was convinced that "Hindus" were not a religious community but a racial group — a "Hindu Race" that possessed the right to dominate India. He believed that European fascism had demonstrated the right to define nationality by race and proved how "every Race" possesses the "right of excommunicating from its Nationality" all those who have "turned traitors" by holding aspirations different from those of the "National Race."

"Different aspirations" meant, simply, not being a Hindu. He accused converts away from Hinduism of changing their "national identity" and betraying the "spirit of love and devotion to the nation." He declared that the only "nationalist patriots" are those who "glorify the Hindu Race and Nation" and that all others in the country are "traitors" who have joined the "camp of the enemy" and left their "mother-nation in the lurch."

He described non-Hindus like Christians and Muslims as "internal threats" and members of "foreign races" who were infected by a "foreign mental complexion," had failed to "merge in the common stream of our national life," and must be stripped of citizen's rights.

And he praised Nazi Germany for protecting its racial and cultural purity by "purging the country of the Semitic races — the Jews." Calling it "race pride" manifested at its highest, he pointed to the purge as an example of how different "races and cultures" cannot be "assimilated into one united whole." And he called it a "good lesson for us… to learn and profit by."

That's the ideology of the RSS, the fascist paramilitary whose six million or more members include Narendra Modi, Amit Shah, and 75 percent of India's cabinet ministers.

That's the ideology which motivates BJP leaders to

shout "shoot the traitors" as people pack the streets of India to protest efforts to turn the country into a religious apartheid state.

That's the ideology which has set Delhi on fire over the last week.

Delhi has been burning since the 23rd of February, when a BJP leader instigated mobs to take to the streets to disperse the peaceful anti-CAA demonstrators who have spent over two months occupying public spaces all around the city in continuous, 24/7 sit-in protests.

Now, blood flows in the streets of Delhi as the city is swallowed up by violence. Muslims are being systematically hunted down, dragged from their homes, beaten black and blue to be left lying in the gutter — even publicly tortured by police as they're forced to sing the National Anthem. Mosques are burning as thugs climb their minarets to raise the saffron flag of the RSS.

More than 40 people lie dead from the worst communal violence in the country's capital since the 1984 Sikh Genocide. Their killers are proudly raising the same slogan we heard during the 2002 Gujarat Pogrom: "The police are with us."

"What happened in Delhi was a pogrom," says journalist Mira Kamdar. "Mobs targeting a single religious group were allowed to run riot, unchecked by police. That is the definition of a pogrom."

No longer is Modi merely the "Butcher of Gujarat" — under the reign of his RSS regime, he has become the Butcher of India.

"India is descending into a night of dread and despair," says Indian political scientist Pratap Bhanu Mehta. "The ongoing riots in Delhi are not a tactical aberration, some absent-minded lapse of attention. They have been in the making for a while, and represent the future that our ruling classes, with our aid and support, have imagined for us. The idea is to carpet bomb the Indian republic as we know it, and replace it with a regime that thrives on cruelty, fear, division, and violence."

Fascism is not rising in India — it has risen.

And the threat of genocide looms large.

Here in America, sitting literally on the other side of the world, we face a choice.

Will we just watch and wait for the next pogrom, for the next genocide warning, for the next community to be "othered," targeted, and systematically exterminated?

Will we just watch and wait for the Indian version of "Schindler's List" to hit the silver screen so that we can take a couple hours on a Saturday evening to munch popcorn as we shed crocodile tears and wring our hands, asking, "How could it have happened?"

Will we imitate the Americans of the 1930s and remain mute spectators while the fascists abroad use our soil in America to spread their doctrines of hate, violence, and supremacy?

That is exactly what is happening today. Modi's regime is drawing moral and material assistance from a support base in the USA — from the thousands of Indian-Americans who belong to the overseas wings of the RSS and the BJP, who organize his rock-star receptions around America, who fund his campaigns, and who travel to India en masse to work for his election.

Meanwhile, President Trump is busy putting profits over people as he does the dance of love with Modi at his rockstar receptions, negotiates trade deals with him, and then turns around to tell us that Modi "very strongly" wants people to have religious freedom even while the Butcher of

India is sending religious minorities to the graveyard.

Decades from now, will we look back and shake our heads over the travesty and tragedy that the USA supported yet another brutal dictator just as it did with the Shah of Iran, Pinochet in Chile, Suharto in Indonesia, Saddam Hussein in Iraq, the Khmer Rouge in Cambodia, and countless other authoritarian regimes around the globe?

Or will we be silent no longer as we stand against the current of the times to lift up our lamps and provide a flicker of hope that liberty, peace, and prosperity can touch the shores of every nation of the world?

America is unique for at least two reasons.

We have a culture of liberty. Though imperfectly practiced and inconsistently protected, our enumerated rights are correctly understood as inalienable — meaning that they are absolute, non-negotiable, and cannot be taken away. Flowing from our Creator, our rights exist not by some whim of the government but by virtue of our very own existence.

We are also a land of refugees. The sole purpose of America's existence is to provide refuge for the tired, the poor, the wretched, the homeless, the huddled masses yearning to be free. From the day that the Mayflower first landed at Plymouth Rock all the way to the present day, every resident of America ended up here as a refugee in some way or another — whether they arrived in search of freedom from religious, economic, social, or political persecution, every American in America is here because it is the land of opportunity. The opportunity to be free.

But our freedom doesn't exist so that we can grow rich and fat and arrogant. Our rights are accompanied by a single sacred duty — the duty to speak out against tyranny and show all other nations of the world that they, too, can be free. For those of us gathered here today, the first and best way to do that is to be a voice for the voiceless persecuted people of India — for the widows who are thrown behind bars because their daughters dared to stare fascism in the face.

Let us remember that our silence in the face of oppression means that we have chosen the side of the oppressor — and let us not fail at our duty to speak.

You must speak out.

Originally presented as a speech at the seminar "Dark Clouds Over South Asia" organized in Newark, California by Dr. Nazeer Ahmed.

— Acknowledgements —

I owe a great deal of gratitude to the the patient and insightful editors who helped me polish many of the pieces included in this publication, including: Eric Garris, Helen Pluckrose, Francesca Recchia, and Siddharth Varadarajan. If I have not mentioned your name, it is only out of concern for your security. To all, my greatest appreciation for your suggestions, advice, and guidance as many of these pieces were brought to publication.

— About the Author —

Pieter Friedrich is a freelance journalist specializing in analysis of South Asian affairs. A native of California, he is the co-author of several books and reports. A frequent speaker at universities, seminars, and protests, he engages with issues such as human rights, supremacist political ideologies, ethno-nationalism, politicization of religion, authoritarian government structures and policies, state-sponsored atrocities, and the need to unify around doctrines of liberty and a politics of reconciliation rather than hate.

Printed in Great Britain
by Amazon